Min

Guitar
Chord
Dictionary

All the essential chords in
an easy-to-follow format!

Alfred Music Co., Inc.
P.O. Box 10003
Van Nuys, CA 91410-0003
alfred.com

ISBN-10: 0-7390-9528-5
ISBN-13: 978-0-7390-9528-7

Cover guitar photos courtesy of Gibson USA and Fender Musical Instruments.

 Alfred Cares. Contents printed on environmentally responsible paper.

Contents

3

Introduction

Alfred's Mini Music Guide *Guitar Chord Dictionary* provides the most essential chords and chordal information in a portable, handy size, and it is loaded with a variety of fingerings for the most important chords in all 12 keys.

Starting on page 19, the chords are listed alphabetically and chromatically for quick reference (A♭, A, B♭, B, etc.). On each page, the chord fingerings are arranged in a logical order, starting from the lowest position on the fingerboard to the highest. Within each key, the chords progress from the most basic major and minor chords all the way up to 7ths, 9ths, and even altered chords.

For each chord, there is an illustrated chord diagram with fingerings and note names; see page 18 for an explanation of how to read these.

The first part of this book (pages 5–18) makes it easy to understand intervals and how chords are constructed. Theory on triads, seventh chords, extended chords, altered chords, and other chord types are covered.

You can refer to the section on moveable barre chords (starting on page 211), which will maximize your knowledge by showing how to play 12 different chords with a single fingering. Once you understand basic chord theory and the concept of moveable barre chords, you can take the chords in this book and use them to fit any performance situation. *Guitar Chord Dictionary* provides the basis for an ever-growing chord vocabulary that can be applied in all musical styles.

Have fun!

Chord Theory

Intervals

Play any note on the guitar, then play a note one fret above it. The distance between these two notes is a *half step*. Play another note followed by a note two frets above it. The distance between these two notes is a *whole step* (two half steps). The distance between any two notes is referred to as an *interval*.

In the example of the C major scale below, the letter names are shown above the notes and the *scale degrees* (numbers) of the notes are written below. Notice that C is the first degree of the scale, D is the second, etc.

The name of an interval is determined by counting the number of scale degrees from one note to the next. For example, an interval of a 3rd, starting on C, would be determined by counting up three scale degrees, or C–D–E (1–2–3). C to E is a 3rd. An interval of a 4th, starting on C, would be determined by counting up four scale degrees, or C–D–E–F (1–2–3–4). C to F is a 4th.

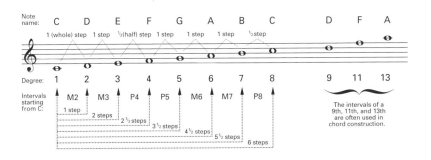

As shown on the previous page, intervals are not only labeled by the distance between scale degrees, but by the *quality* of the interval. An interval's quality is determined by counting the number of whole steps and half steps between the two notes of an interval. For example, C to E is a 3rd. C to E is also a major third because there are two whole steps between C and E. Likewise, C to E♭ is a 3rd, but C to E♭ is also a minor third because there are 1½ steps between C and E♭. There are five qualities used to describe intervals: *major, minor, perfect, diminished,* and *augmented.* Following are abbreviations for the different interval qualities.

M	= Major	o	= Diminished (dim)
m	= Minor	+	= Augmented (aug)
P	= Perfect		

Particular intervals are associated with certain qualities:

2nds, 9ths	=	Major, Minor, and Augmented
3rds, 6ths, 13ths	=	Major, Minor, Augmented, and Diminished
4ths, 5ths, 11ths	=	Perfect, Augmented, and Diminished
7ths	=	Major, Minor, and Diminished

When a major interval is made *smaller* by a half step it becomes a minor interval.

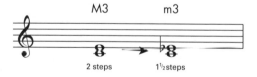

When a minor interval is made *larger* by a half step it becomes a major interval.

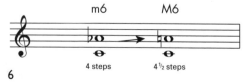

When a minor or perfect interval is made *smaller* by a half step it becomes a diminished interval.

When a major or perfect interval is made *larger* by a half step it becomes an augmented interval.

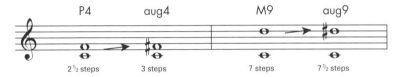

Below is a table of intervals starting on the note C. Notice that some intervals are labeled *enharmonic*, which means they are written differently but sound the same (see aug2 and m3).

Table of Intervals

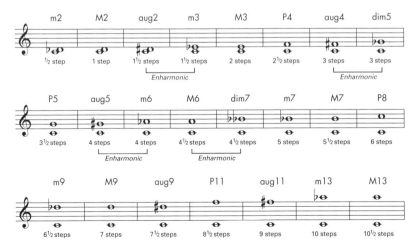

Basic Triads

A *chord* consists of two or more notes played together. Most commonly, a chord will have three or more notes. A three-note chord is called a *triad*. The *root* of a triad (or any other chord) is the note from which a chord is constructed. The relationship of the intervals from the root to the other notes of a chord determines the chord *type*. Triads are most frequently identified as one of four chord types: *major*, *minor*, *diminished*, and *augmented*.

All chord types can be identified by the intervals used to create the chord. For example, the C major triad is built beginning with C as the root, adding a major 3rd (E), and adding a perfect 5th (G). All major triads contain a root, M3, and P5.

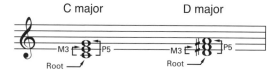

Minor triads contain a root, minor 3rd, and perfect 5th. (An easier way to build a minor triad is to simply lower the 3rd of a major triad.) All minor triads contain a root, m3, and P5.

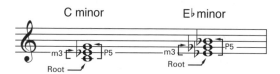

Diminished triads contain a root, minor 3rd, and diminished 5th. If the perfect 5th of a minor triad is made smaller by a half step (to become a diminished 5th), the result is a diminished triad. All diminished triads contain a root, m3, and dim5.

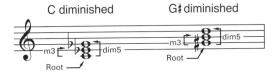

Augmented triads contain a root, major 3rd, and augmented 5th. If the perfect 5th of a major triad is made larger by a half step (to become an augmented 5th), the result is an augmented triad. All augmented triads contain a root, M3, and aug5.

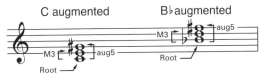

An important concept to remember about chords is that the bottom note of a chord will *not* always be the root. If the root of a triad, for instance, is moved above the 5th so that the 3rd is the bottom note of the chord, it is said to be in the *first inversion*. If the root and 3rd are moved above the 5th, the chord is in the *second inversion*. The number of inversions that a chord can have is related to the number of notes in the chord: a three-note chord can have two inversions, a four-note chord can have three inversions, etc.

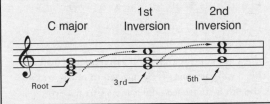

Building Chords

By using the four chord types as basic building blocks, it is possible to create a variety of chords by adding 6ths, 7ths, 9ths, and even 11ths and 13ths. Following are examples of some of the many variations.

* The *suspended fourth* chord does not contain a third. An assumption is made that the 4th degree of the chord will harmonically be inclined to *resolve* to the 3rd degree. In other words, the 4th is *suspended* until it moves to the 3rd.

Up until now, the examples have shown intervals and chord construction based on C. Until you are familiar with all the chords, the C chord examples on the previous pages can serve as a reference guide when building chords based on other notes: For instance, locate C7(♭9). To construct a G7(♭9) chord, first determine what intervals are contained in C7(♭9), then follow the steps outlined on the next page.

C Seventh Flat Ninth
C7(♭9)

C Seventh Flat Ninth
C7(♭9)

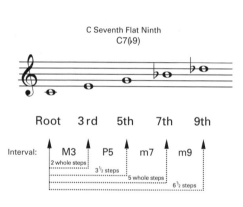

Now, let's figure out how to construct a G7(♭9) chord:

1. Determine the root of the chord. A chord is always named for its root—in this case, G is the root of G7(♭9).

2. Count letter names up from the letter name of the root (G), as we did when building intervals on page 4, to determine the intervals of the chord. Counting three letter names up from G to B (G–A–B, 1–2–3) is a 3rd, G to D (G–A–B–C–D) is a 5th, G to F is a 7th, and G to A is a 9th.

3. Determine the quality of the intervals by counting whole steps and half steps up from the root; G to B (2 whole steps) is a major 3rd, G to D (3½ steps) is a perfect 5th, G to F (5 whole steps) is a minor 7th, and G to A♭ (6½ steps) is a minor 9th.

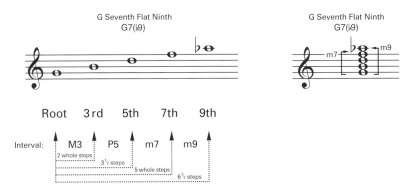

Follow this general guideline to figure out the notes of any chord. As interval and chord construction become more familiar, it will become possible to create your own original fingerings on the guitar. Feel free to experiment!

The Circle of 5ths

Guitar Chord Dictionary is organized to provide the fingerings of chords in all keys. The *circle of 5ths* below will help to clarify which chords are enharmonic equivalents (notice that chords can be written enharmonically as well as notes, see page 7). The circle of 5ths also serves as a quick reference guide to the relationship of the keys and how key signatures can be figured out. Clockwise movement (up a P5) provides all of the sharp keys by adding one sharp to the key signature. Counterclockwise (down a P5) provides the flat keys by adding one flat.

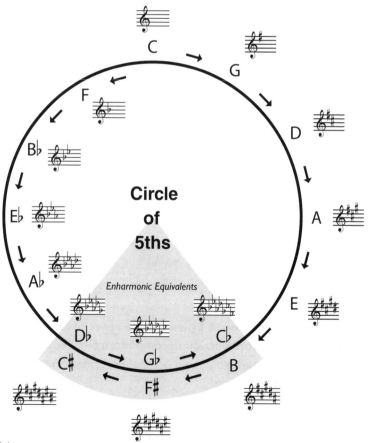

Reading Chords
Chord Symbol Variations

Chord symbols are a form of musical shorthand that give the guitarist as much information about a chord as quickly as possible. Since chord symbols are not universally standardized, they are often written in many different ways—some are understandable, others are confusing. To illustrate this point, below is a listing of some of the ways copyists, composers, and arrangers have created variations on the more common chord symbols.

C	Csus	C(♭5)	C(add9)
C major Cmaj CM	Csus4 C(addF) C4	C-5 C(5-) C(♯4)	C(9) C(add2) C(+9) C(+D)

C5	Cm	C+	C°
C(no3) C(omit3)	Cmin Cmi C-	C+5 Caug Caug5 C(♯5)	C° C°7 C7°

C6	C6/9	Cm6/9	Cm6
Cmaj6 C(addA) C(A)	C6(add9) C6(addD) C9(no7) C9/6	C-6/9 Cm6(+9) Cm6(add9) Cm6(+D)	C-6 Cm(addA) Cm(+6)

C7	C7sus	Cm7	Cm7($\flat$5)
C(addB$\flat$) C7̶ C(-7) C(+7)	C7sus4 Csus7 C7(+4)	Cmi7 Cmin7 C-7 C7mi	Cmi7-5 C-7(5-) Cø C ½dim

C7+	C7($\flat$5)	Cmaj7	Cmaj7($\flat$5)
C7+5 C7aug C7aug5 C7($\sharp$5)	C7-5 C7(5-) C7̶-5 C7($\sharp$4)	Cma7 C7̶ C△ C△7	Cmaj7(-5) C7̶(-5) C△($\flat$5)

Cm(maj7)	C7($\flat$9)	C7($\sharp$9)	C7+($\flat$9)
C-maj7 C-7̶ Cmi7̶	C7(-9) C9$\flat$ C9-	C7(+9) C9$\sharp$ C9+	Caug7-9 C+7($\flat$9) C+9$\flat$ C7+(-9)

Cm9	C9	C9+	C9(♭5)
Cm7(9) Cm7(+9) C-9 Cmi7(9+)	$C7^{9}$ C7add9 C7(addD) C7(+9)	C9(+5) Caug9 C(♯9♯5) C+9	C9(-5) $C7^{9}_{-5}$ C9(5♭)

Cmaj9	C9(♯11)	Cm9(maj7)	C11
C$\overline{7}$(9) C$\overline{7}$(+9) C9(maj7) C$\overline{9}$	C9(+11) C(♯11) C11+ C11♯	C-9(♯7) C(-9)$\overline{7}$ Cmi9(♯7)	C9(11) C9addF C9+11 $C7^{9}_{11}$

Cm11	C13	C13(♭9)	C13($^{♭9}_{♭5}$)
C-11 Cm(♭11) Cmi7$^{11}_{9}$ C-7($^{9}_{11}$)	C9addA C9(6) C7addA C7+A	C13(-9) $C^{13}_{♭9}$ C(♭9)addA	C13(-9-5) C(♭9♭5)addA

Chord Frames

Guitar *chord frames* are diagrams that contain all the information necessary to play a particular chord. The fingerings, note names, and position of the chord on the neck are all provided on the chord frame (see below). The photo to the right shows which number corresponds to which fretting-hand finger.

Choose chord positions that require the least motion from one chord to the next; select fingerings that are in approximately the same location on the guitar neck. This will provide smoother and more comfortable transitions between chords in a progression.

The following illustrations explain the various chord frame symbols.

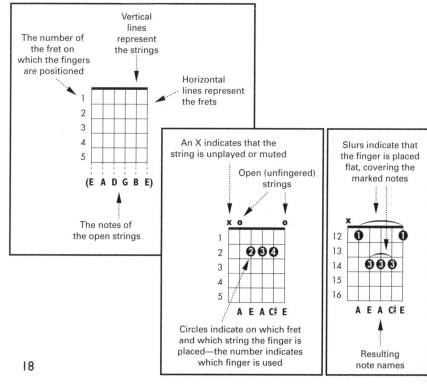

Chords in All 12 Keys

A♭

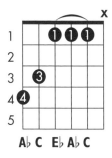

A♭ C E♭ A♭ C

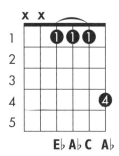

E♭ A♭ C A♭

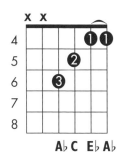

A♭ C E♭ A♭

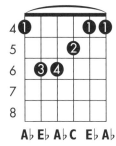

A♭ E♭ A♭ C E♭ A♭

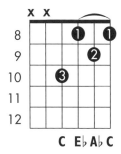

C E♭ A♭ C

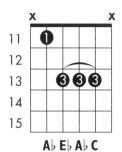

A♭ E♭ A♭ C

A♭m

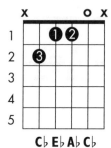

C♭ E♭ A♭ C♭

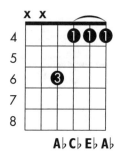

A♭ C♭ E♭ A♭

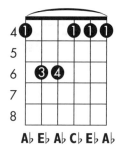

A♭ E♭ A♭ C♭ E♭ A♭

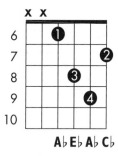

A♭ E♭ A♭ C♭

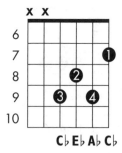

C♭ E♭ A♭ C♭

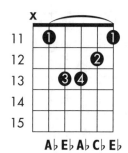

A♭ E♭ A♭ C♭ E♭

A♭+

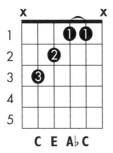

C E A♭ C

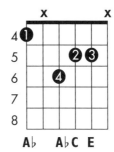

A♭   A♭ C E

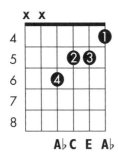

A♭ C E A♭

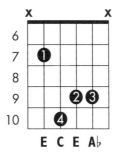

E C E A♭

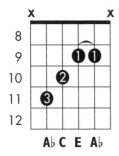

A♭ C E A♭

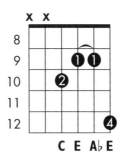

C E A♭ E

Absus4

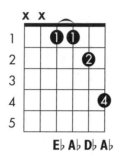

Eb Ab Db Ab

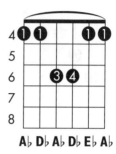

Ab Db Ab Db Eb Ab

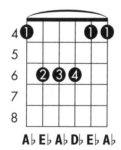

Ab Eb Ab Db Eb Ab

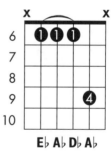

Eb Ab Db Ab

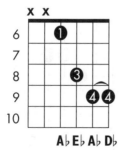

Ab Eb Ab Db

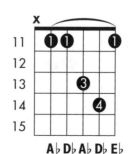

Ab Db Ab Db Eb

Ab5

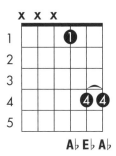

Ab Eb Ab

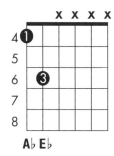

Ab Eb

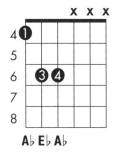

Ab Eb Ab

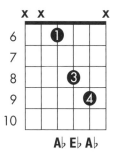

Ab Eb Ab

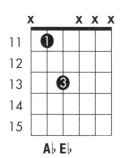

Ab Eb Ab

Ab Eb

Ab6

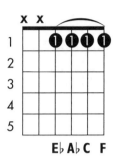

E♭ A♭ C F

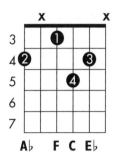

A♭ F C E♭

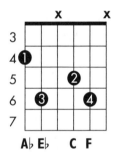

A♭ E♭ C F

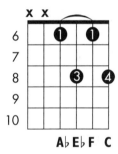

A♭ E♭ F C

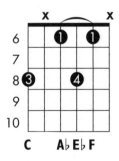

C A♭ E♭ F

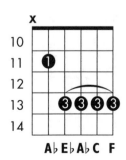

A♭ E♭ A♭ C F

A♭m6

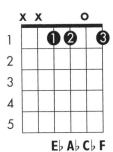

E♭ A♭ C♭ F

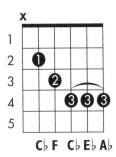

C♭ F C♭ E♭ A♭

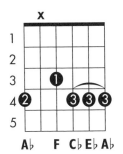

A♭ F C♭ E♭ A♭

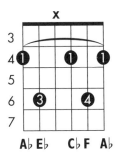

A♭ E♭ C♭ F A♭

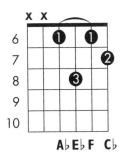

A♭ E♭ F C♭

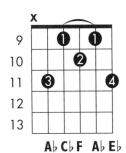

A♭ C♭ F A♭ E♭

25

Ab7

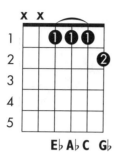

Eb Ab C Gb

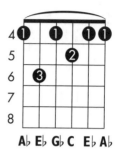

Ab Eb Gb C Eb Ab

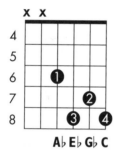

Ab Eb Gb C

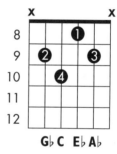

Gb C Eb Ab

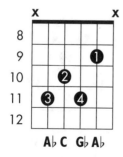

Ab C Gb Ab

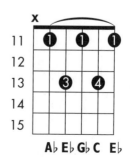

Ab Eb Gb C Eb

26

A♭maj7

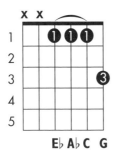

E♭ A♭ C G

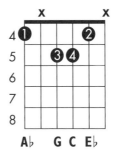

A♭ G C E♭

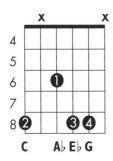

C A♭ E♭ G

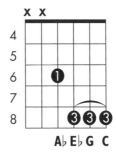

A♭ E♭ G C

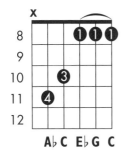

A♭ C E♭ G C

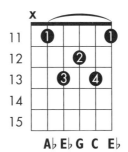

A♭ E♭ G C E♭

A♭m7

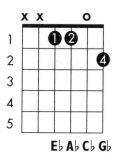

E♭ A♭ C♭ G♭

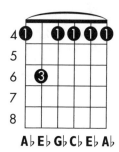

A♭ E♭ G♭ C♭ E♭ A♭

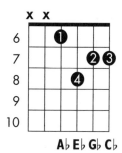

A♭ E♭ G♭ C♭

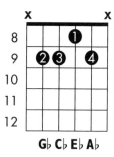

G♭ C♭ E♭ A♭

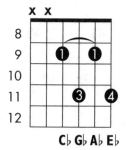

C♭ G♭ A♭ E♭

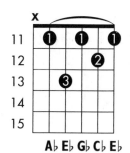

A♭ E♭ G♭ C♭ E♭

A♭

A♭m7(♭5)

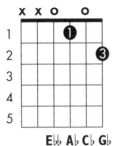

E♭♭ A♭ C♭ G♭

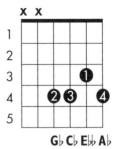

G♭ C♭ E♭♭ A♭

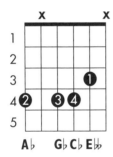

A♭ G♭ C♭ E♭♭

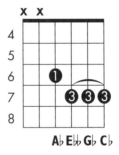

A♭ E♭♭ G♭ C♭

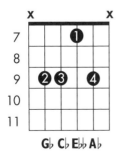

G♭ C♭ E♭♭ A♭

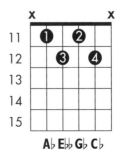

A♭ E♭♭ G♭ C♭

A♭

A♭°7

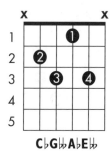

C♭G♭♭A♭E♭♭

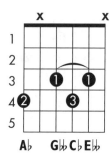

A♭　G♭♭C♭E♭♭

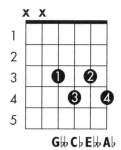

G♭♭C♭E♭♭A♭

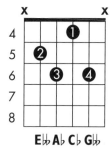

E♭♭A♭C♭G♭♭

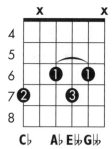

C♭　A♭E♭♭G♭♭

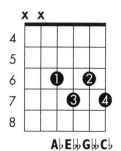

A♭E♭♭G♭♭C♭

A♭9

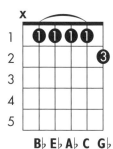

B♭ E♭ A♭ C G♭

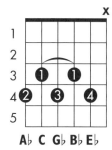

A♭ C G♭ B♭ E♭

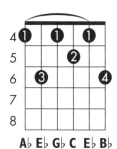

A♭ E♭ G♭ C E♭ B♭

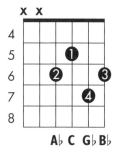

A♭ C G♭ B♭

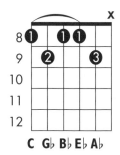

C G♭ B♭ E♭ A♭

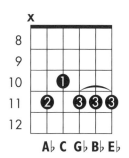

A♭ C G♭ B♭ E♭

A♭maj9

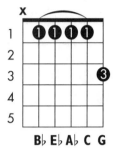

B♭ E♭ A♭ C G

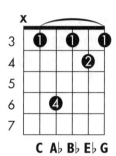

C A♭ B♭ E♭ G

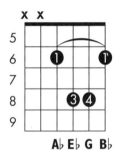

A♭ E♭ G B♭

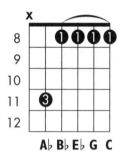

A♭ B♭ E♭ G C

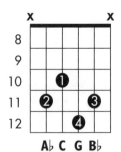

A♭ C G B♭

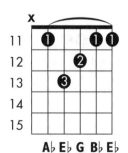

A♭ E♭ G B♭ E♭

A♭m9

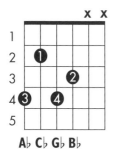

A♭ C♭ G♭ B♭

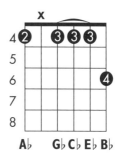

A♭ G♭ C♭ E♭ B♭

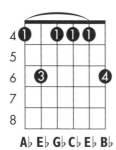

A♭ E♭ G♭ C♭ E♭ B♭

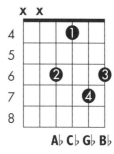

A♭ C♭ G♭ B♭

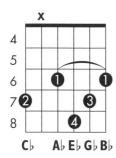

C♭ A♭ E♭ G♭ B♭

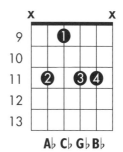

A♭ C♭ G♭ B♭

A♭

33

Ab

Abmaj7(b5)

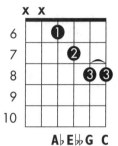

A♭ E♭♭ G C

Ab7(b5)

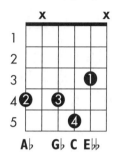

A♭ G♭ C E♭♭

Ab7+

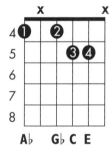

A♭ G♭ C E

Ab7(b9)

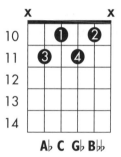

A♭ C G♭ B♭♭

Ab7(#9)

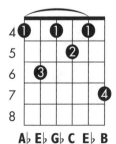

A♭ E♭ G♭ C E♭ B

Ab9(b5)

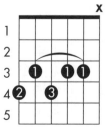

A♭ C G♭ B♭ E♭♭

A

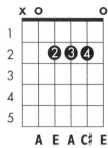

A E A C# E

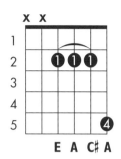

E A C# A

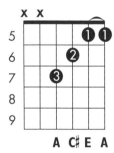

A C# E A

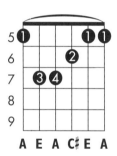

A E A C# E A

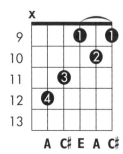

A C# E A C#

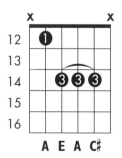

A E A C#

Am

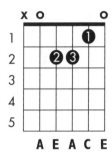

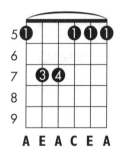

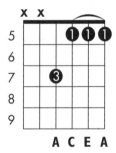

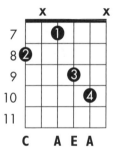

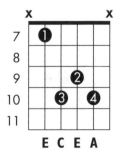

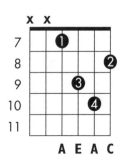

A+

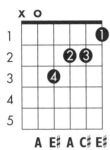

A E♯ A C♯ E♯

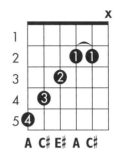

A C♯ E♯ A C♯

A

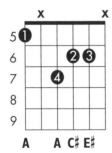

A   A C♯ E♯

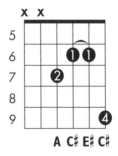

A C♯ E♯ C♯

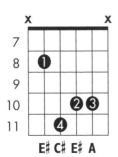

E♯ C♯ E♯ A

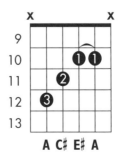

A C♯ E♯ A

Asus4

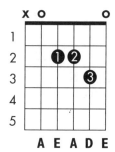

A E A D E

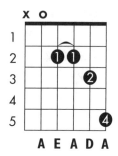

A E A D A

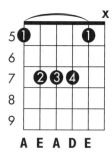

A E A D E

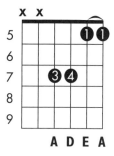

A D E A

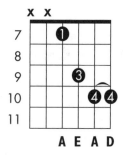

A E A D

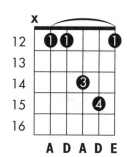

A D A D E

A5

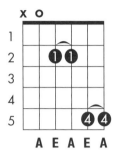

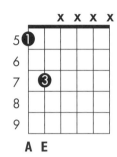

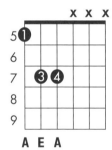

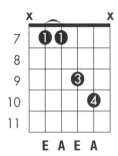

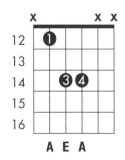

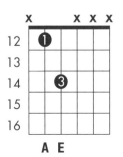

A

39

A6

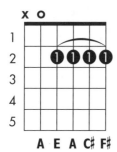

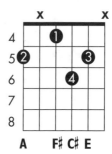

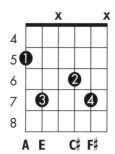

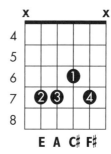

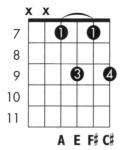

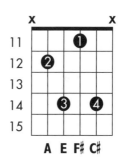

Am6

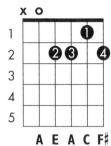

A E A C F#

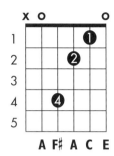

A F# A C E

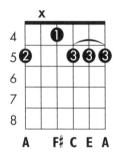

A F# C E A

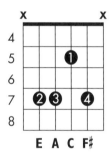

E A C F#

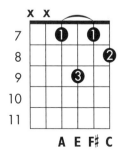

A E F# C

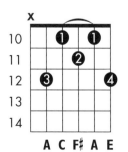

A C F# A E

A7

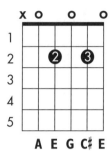

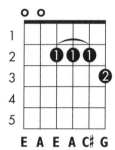

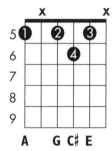

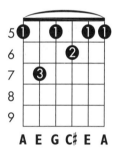

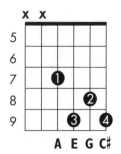

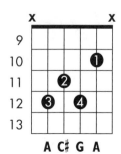

Amaj7

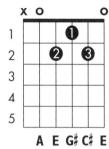

A E G# C# E

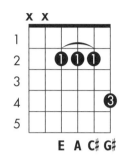

E A C# G#

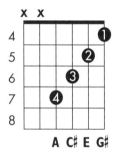

A C# E G#

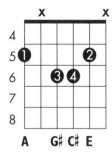

A G# C# E

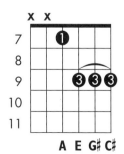

A E G# C#

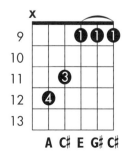

A C# E G# C#

A

Am7

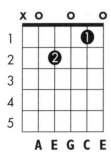

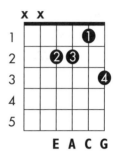

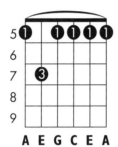

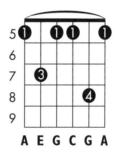

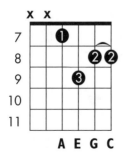

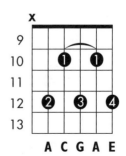

Am7(♭5)

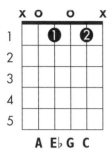

A E♭ G C

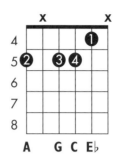

A G C E♭

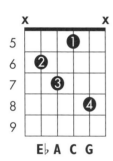

E♭ A C G

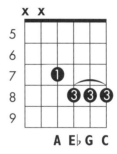

A E♭ G C

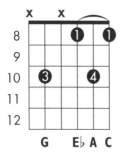

G E♭ A C

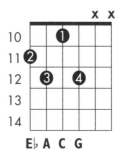

E♭ A C G

A°7

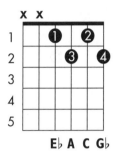

Eb A C Gb

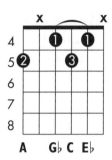

A Gb C Eb

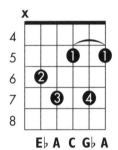

Eb A C Gb A

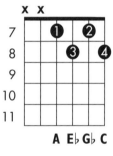

A Eb Gb C

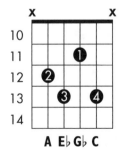

A Eb Gb C

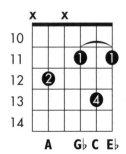

A Gb C Eb

A9

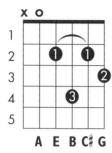

A E B C# G

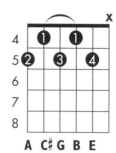

A C# G B E

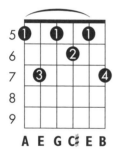

A E G C# E B

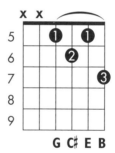

G C# E B

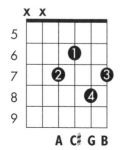

A C# G B

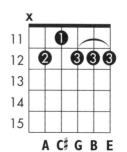

A C# G B E

Amaj9

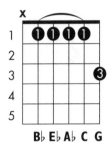

Bb Eb Ab C G

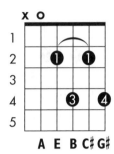

A E B C# G#

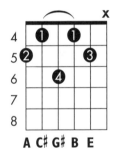

A C# G# B E

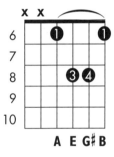

A E G# B

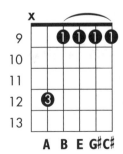

A B E G#C#

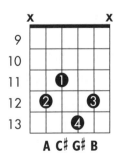

A C# G# B

Am9

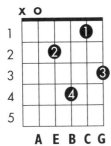

A E B C G

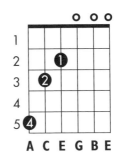

A C E G B E

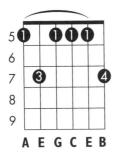

A E G C E B

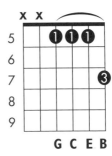

G C E B

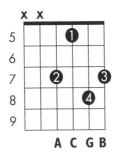

A C G B

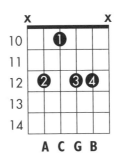

A C G B

Amaj7(♭5)

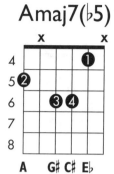

A7(♭5)

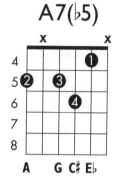

A7+

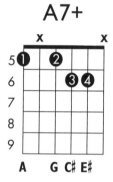

A7(♭9)

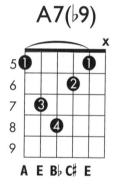

A7(♯9)

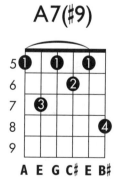

A9(♭5)

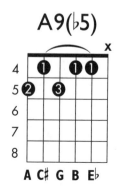

B♭

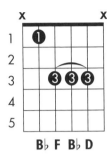

B♭ F B♭ D

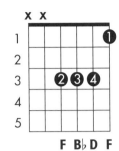

F B♭ D F

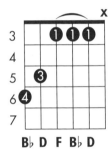

B♭ D F B♭ D

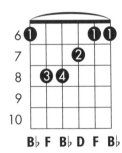

B♭ F B♭ D F B♭

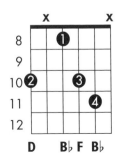

D   B♭ F B♭

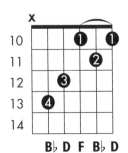

B♭ D F B♭ D

B♭m

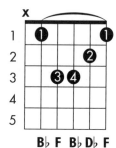

B♭ F B♭ D♭ F

F B♭ D♭ F

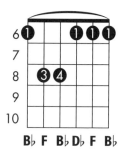

B♭ F B♭ D♭ F B♭

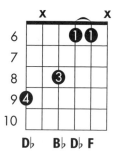

D♭ B♭ D♭ F

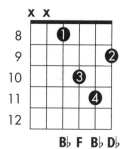

B♭ F B♭ D♭

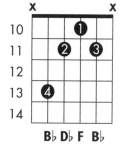

B♭ D♭ F B♭

B♭+

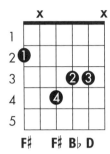

F♯   F♯ B♭ D

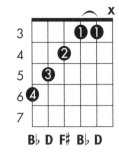

B♭ D F♯ B♭ D

B♭

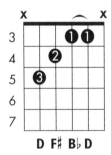

D F♯ B♭ D

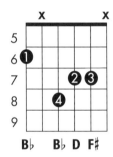

B♭   B♭ D F♯

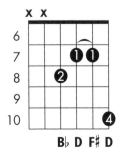

B♭ D F♯ D

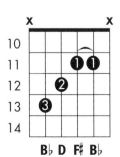

B♭ D F♯ B♭

B♭sus4

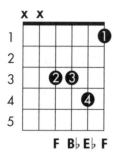

F B♭ E♭ F

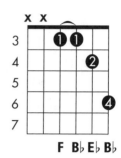

F B♭ E♭ B♭

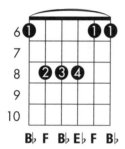

B♭ F B♭ E♭ F B♭

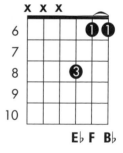

E♭ F B♭

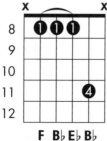

F B♭ E♭ B♭

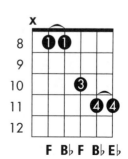

F B♭ F B♭ E♭

B♭5

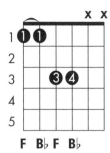

F   B♭ F   B♭

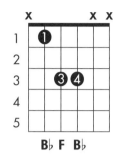

B♭ F   B♭

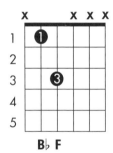

B♭ F

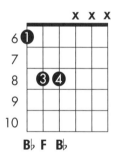

B♭ F   B♭

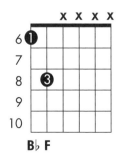

B♭ F

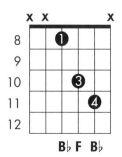

B♭ F   B♭

Bb6

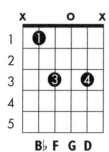

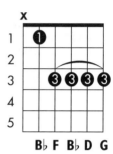

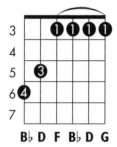

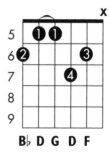

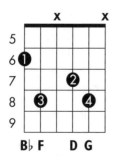

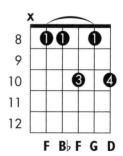

B♭m6

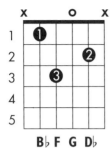

B♭ F G D♭

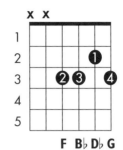

F B♭ D♭ G

B♭

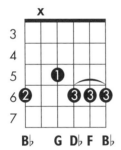

B♭ G D♭ F B♭

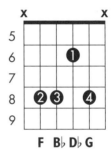

F B♭ D♭ G

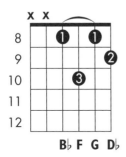

B♭ F G D♭

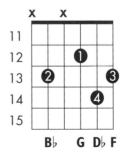

B♭ G D♭ F

Bb7

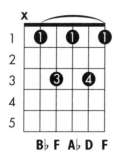

Bb F Ab D F

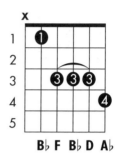

Bb F Bb D Ab

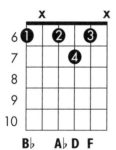

Bb   Ab D F

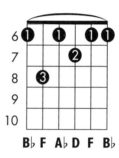

Bb F Ab D F Bb

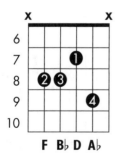

F Bb D Ab

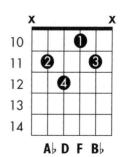

Ab D F Bb

Bb

B♭maj7

B♭ F A D F

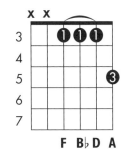

F B♭ D A

B♭

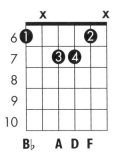

B♭ A D F

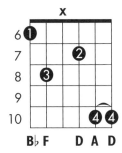

B♭ F D A D

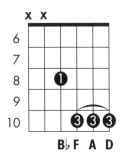

B♭ F A D

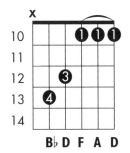

B♭ D F A D

B♭m7

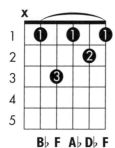

B♭ F A♭ D♭ F

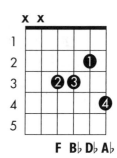

F B♭ D♭ A♭

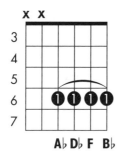

A♭ D♭ F B♭

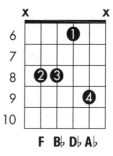

F B♭ D♭ A♭

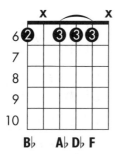

B♭ A♭ D♭ F

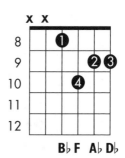

B♭ F A♭ D♭

B♭m7(♭5)

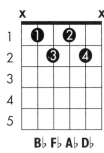

B♭ F♭ A♭ D♭

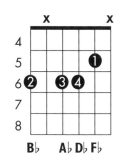

B♭   A♭ D♭ F♭

B♭

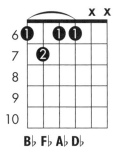

B♭ F♭ A♭ D♭

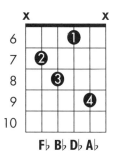

F♭ B♭ D♭ A♭

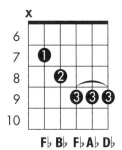

F♭ B♭ F♭A♭ D♭

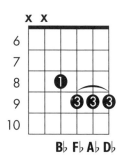

B♭ F♭ A♭ D♭

B♭°7

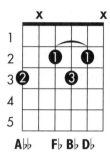

A♭♭   F♭ B♭ D♭

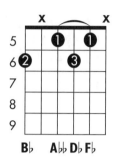

B♭   A♭♭ D♭ F♭

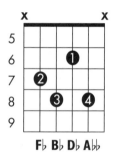

F♭ B♭ D♭ A♭♭

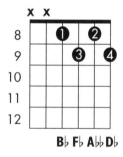

B♭ F♭ A♭♭ D♭

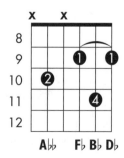

A♭♭   F♭ B♭ D♭

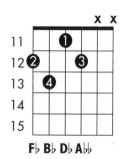

F♭ B♭ D♭ A♭♭

B♭9

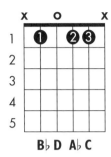

B♭ D A♭ C

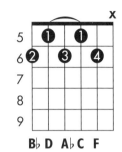

B♭ D A♭ C F

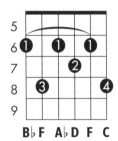

B♭ F A♭ D F C

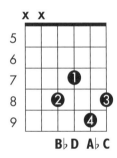

B♭ D A♭ C

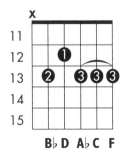

B♭ D A♭ C F

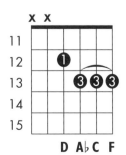

D A♭ C F

B♭

B♭maj9

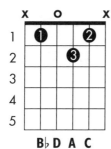

B♭ D A C

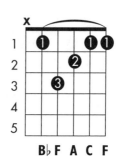

B♭ F A C F

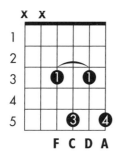

F C D A

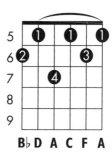

B♭ D A C F A

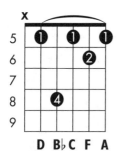

D B♭ C F A

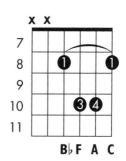

B♭ F A C

B♭

B♭m9

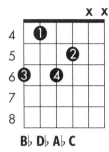

B♭ D♭ A♭ C

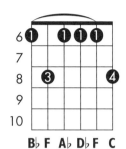

B♭ F A♭ D♭ F C

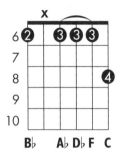

B♭ A♭ D♭ F C

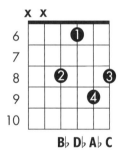

B♭ D♭ A♭ C

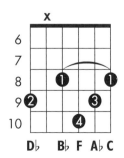

D♭ B♭ F A♭ C

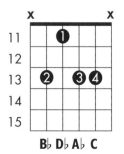

B♭ D♭ A♭ C

B♭maj7(♭5)

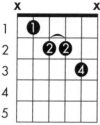

B♭ F♭ A D

B♭7(♭5)

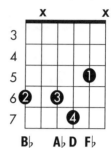

B♭　A♭ D F♭

B♭7+

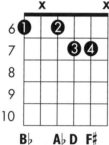

B♭　A♭ D F♯

B♭7(♭9)

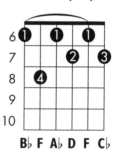

B♭ F A♭ D F C♭

B♭7(♯9)

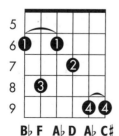

B♭ F　A♭ D A♭ C♯

B♭9(♭5)

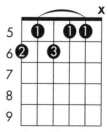

B♭ D A♭ C F♭

B♭

B

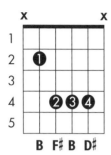

B F♯ B D♯

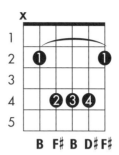

B F♯ B D♯ F♯

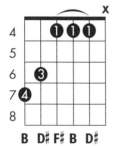

B D♯ F♯ B D♯

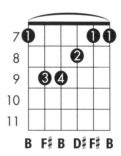

B F♯ B D♯ F♯ B

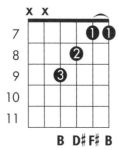

B D♯ F♯ B

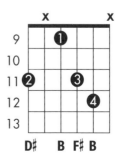

D♯ B F♯ B

Bm

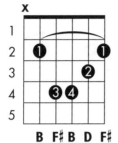

B F# B D F#

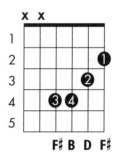

F# B D F#

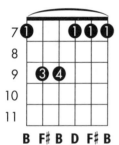

B F# B D F# B

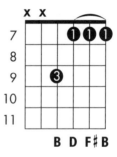

B D F# B

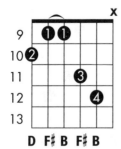

D F# B F# B

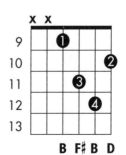

B F# B D

B+

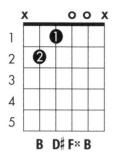

B D♯ F× B

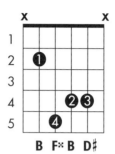

B F× B D♯

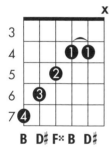

B D♯ F× B D♯

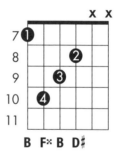

B F× B D♯

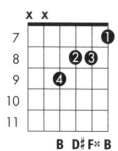

B D♯ F× B

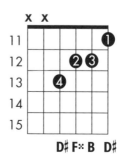

D♯ F× B D♯

Bsus4

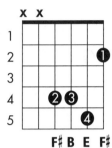

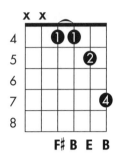

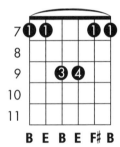

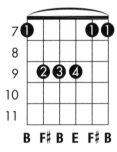

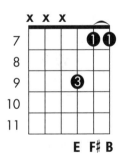

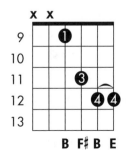

B5

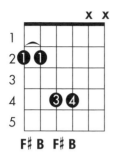

F# B F# B

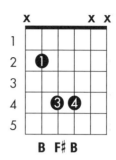

B F# B

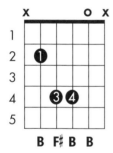

B F# B B

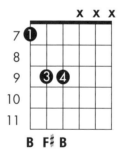

B F# B

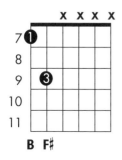

B F#

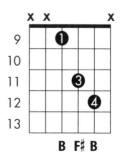

B F# B

B6

B

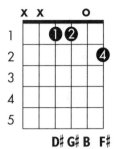

D# G# B F#

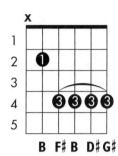

B F# B D# G#

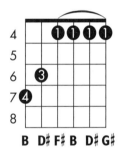

B D# F# B D# G#

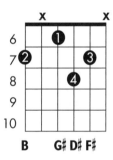

B G# D# F#

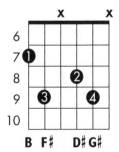

B F# D# G#

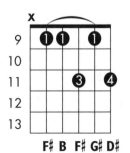

F# B F# G# D#

Bm6

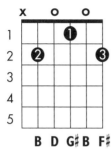

B D G♯ B F♯

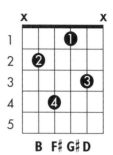

B F♯ G♯ D

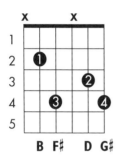

B F♯ D G♯

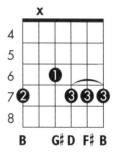

B G♯ D F♯ B

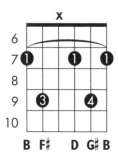

B F♯ D G♯ B

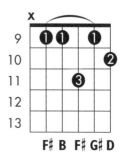

F♯ B F♯ G♯ D

B7

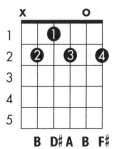

B D# A B F#

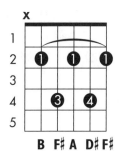

B F# A D# F#

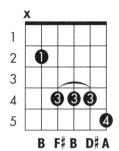

B F# B D# A

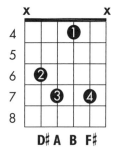

D# A B F#

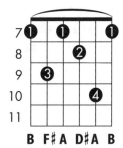

B F# A D# A B

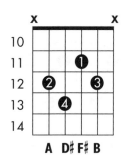

A D# F# B

Bmaj7

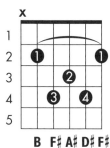

B F# A# D# F#

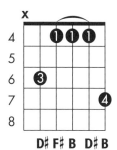

D# F# B D# B

B

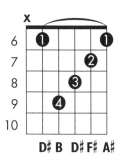

D# B D# F# A#

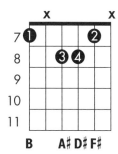

B A# D# F#

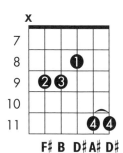

F# B D# A# D#

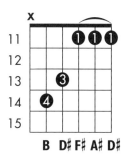

B D# F# A# D#

Bm7

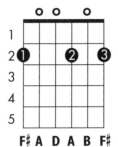

F# A D A B F#

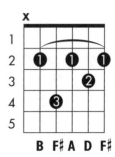

B F# A D F#

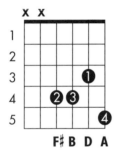

F# B D A

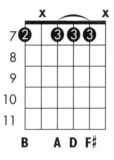

B A D F#

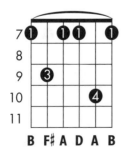

B F# A D A B

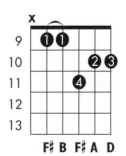

F# B F# A D

Bm7(♭5)

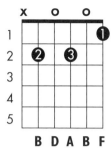

B D A B F

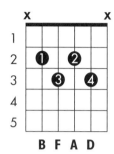

B F A D

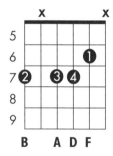

B A D F

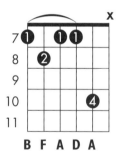

B F A D A

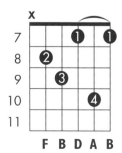

F B D A B

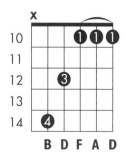

B D F A D

B°7

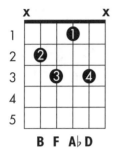

B F A♭ D

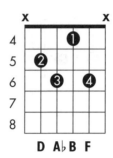

D A♭ B F

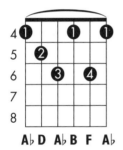

A♭ D A♭ B F A♭

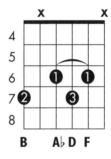

B A♭ D F

D B F A♭

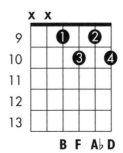

B F A♭ D

B9

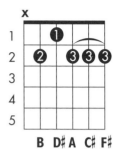

B D#A C#F#

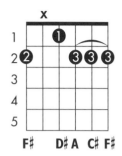

F# D#A C#F#

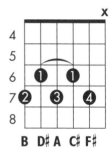

B D#A C#F#

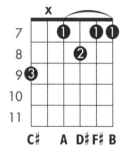

C# A D#F# B

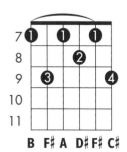

B F#A D#F# C#

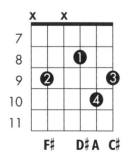

F# D#A C#

Bmaj9

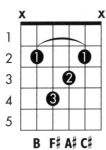

B F# A# C#

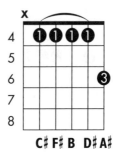

C# F# B D# A#

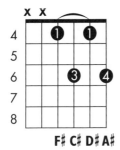

F# C# D# A#

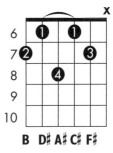

B D# A# C# F#

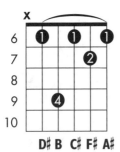

D# B C# F# A#

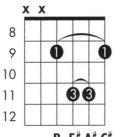

B F# A# C#

Bm9

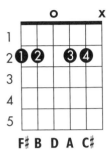

F# B D A C#

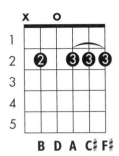

B D A C# F#

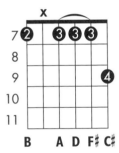

B   A D F# C#

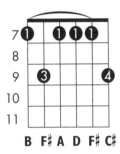

B F# A D F# C#

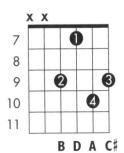

B D A C#

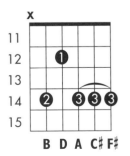

B D A C# F#

B

Bmaj7(♭5)

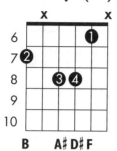

6
7 ②
8 ③ ④
9
10

B   A♯ D♯ F

B7(♭5)

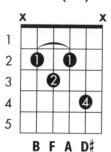

1
2 ① ①
3 ②
4 ④
5

B F A D♯

B7+

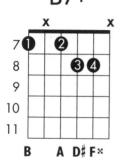

7 ① ②
8 ③ ④
9
10
11

B   A D♯ F✕

B7(♭9)

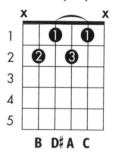

1 ① ①
2 ② ③
3
4
5

B D♯ A C

B7(♯9)

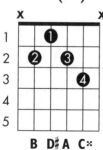

1 ①
2 ② ③
3 ④
4
5

B D♯ A C✕

B9(♭5)

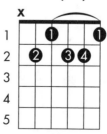

1 ① ①
2 ② ③ ④
3
4
5

B D♯ A C♯ F

B

C

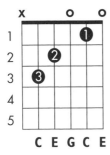

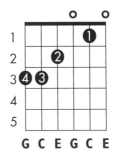

C

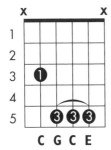

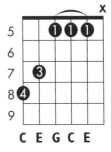

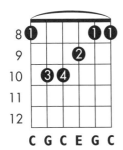

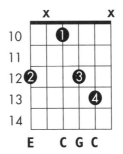

Cm

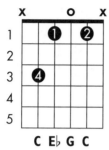

C E♭ G C

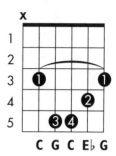

C G C E♭ G

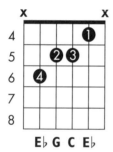

E♭ G C E♭

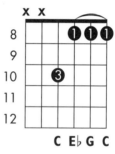

C E♭ G C

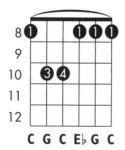

C G C E♭ G C

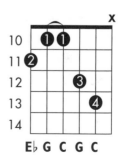

E♭ G C G C

C+

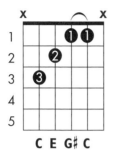

C E G# C

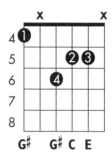

G# G# C E

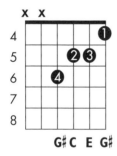

G# C E G#

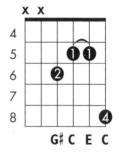

G# C E C

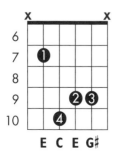

E C E G#

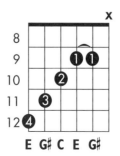

E G# C E G#

C

85

Csus4

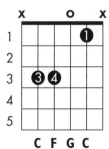

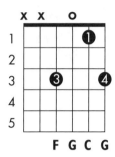

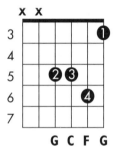

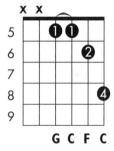

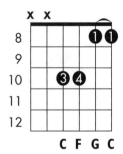

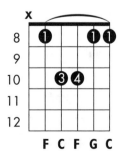

C5

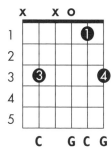

C G C G

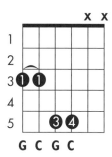

G C G C

C

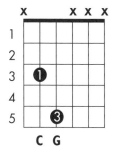

C G

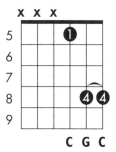

C G C

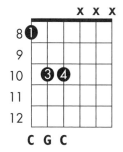

C G C

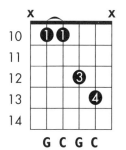

G C G C

C6

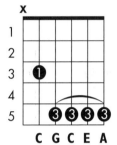

C G C E A

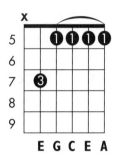

E G C E A

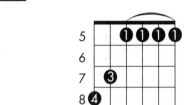

C E G C E A

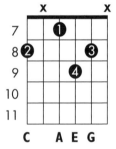

C A E G

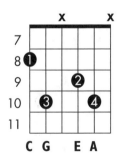

C G E A

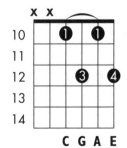

C G A E

Cm6

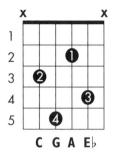

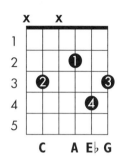

C

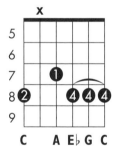

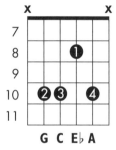

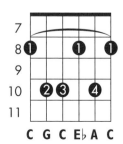

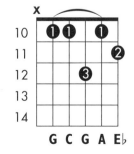

C7

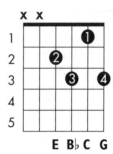

C E B♭ C E

E B♭ C G

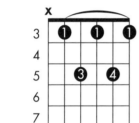
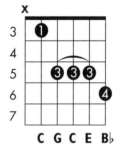

C G B♭ E G

C G C E B♭

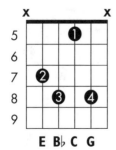
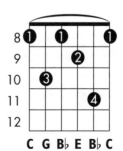

E B♭ C G

C G B♭ E B♭ C

C

Cmaj7

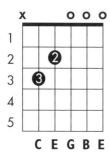

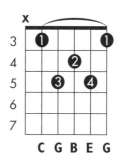

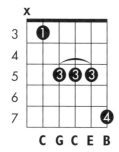

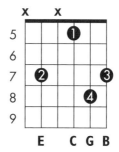

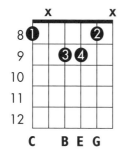

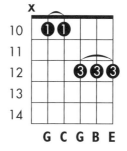

C

Cm7

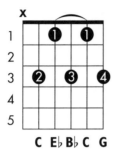

C E♭ B♭ C G

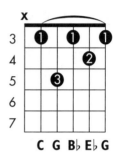

C G B♭ E♭ G

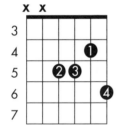

G C E♭ B♭

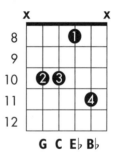

G C E♭ B♭

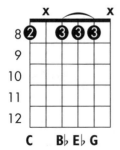

C B♭ E♭ G

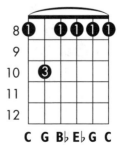

C G B♭ E♭ G C

C

Cm7(♭5)

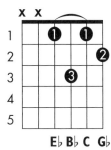

Eb Bb C Gb

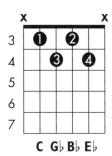

C Gb Bb Eb

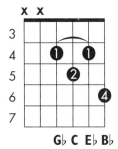

Gb C Eb Bb

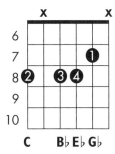

C   Bb Eb Gb

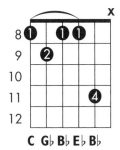

C Gb Bb Eb Bb

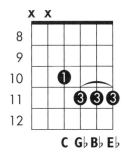

C Gb Bb Eb

C

C°7

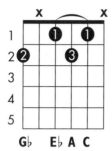

Gb Eb A C

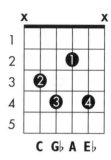

C Gb A Eb

C

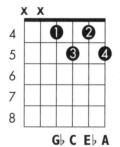

Gb C Eb A

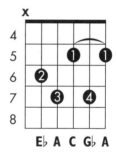

Eb A C Gb A

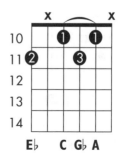

A Eb Gb C

Eb C Gb A

C9

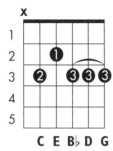

C E B♭ D G

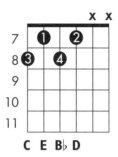

C E B♭ D

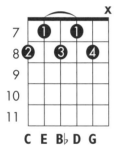

C E B♭ D G

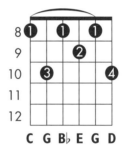

C G B♭ E G D

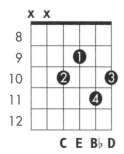

C E B♭ D

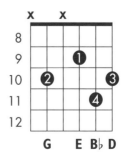

G E B♭ D

C

Cmaj9

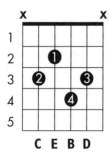

C E B D

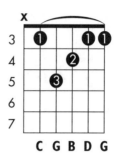

C G B D G

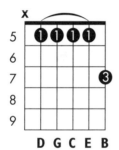

D G C E B

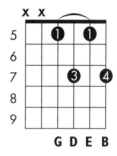

G D E B

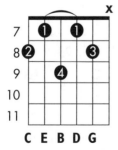

C E B D G

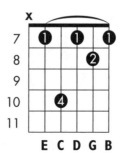

E C D G B

C

Cm9

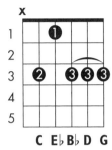

C E♭ B♭ D G

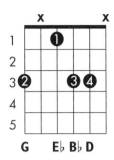

G E♭ B♭ D

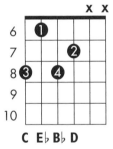

C E♭ B♭ D

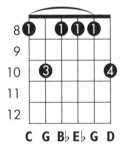

C G B♭ E♭ G D

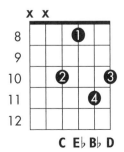

C E♭ B♭ D

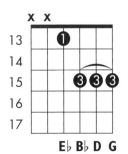

E♭ B♭ D G

C

Cmaj7(♭5)

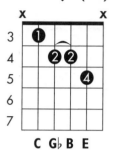

C G♭ B E

C7(♭5)

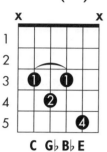

C G♭ B♭ E

C7+

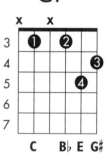

C B♭ E G#

C7(♭9)

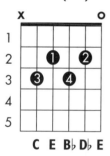

C E B♭ D♭ E

C7(#9)

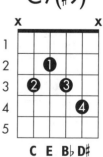

C E B♭ D#

C9(♭5)

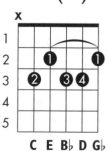

C E B♭ D G♭

D♭

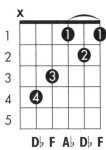

D♭ F A♭ D♭ F

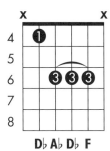

D♭ A♭ D♭ F

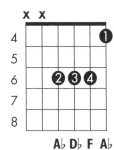

A♭ D♭ F A♭

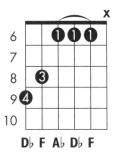

D♭ F A♭ D♭ F

D♭

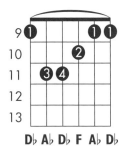

D♭ A♭ D♭ F A♭ D♭

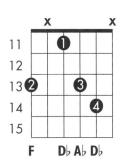

F   D♭ A♭ D♭

D♭m

F♭ A♭ D♭ F♭

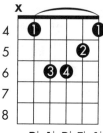

D♭ A♭ D♭ F♭ A♭

D♭

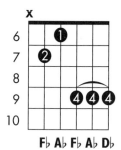

F♭ A♭ F♭ A♭ D♭

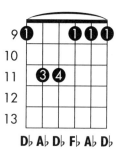

D♭ A♭ D♭ F♭ A♭ D♭

F♭ A♭ D♭ A♭ D♭

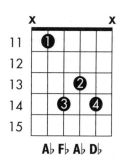

A♭ F♭ A♭ D♭

D♭+

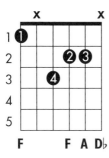

F   F A D♭

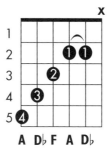

A D♭ F A D♭

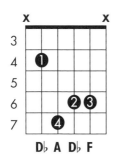

D♭ A D♭ F

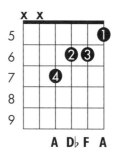

A D♭ F A

D♭

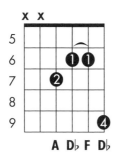

A D♭ F D♭

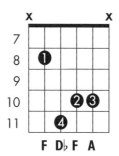

F D♭ F A

101

D♭sus4

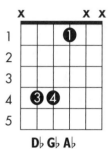

D♭ G♭ A♭

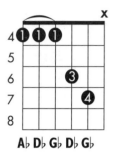

A♭ D♭ G♭ D♭ G♭

D♭

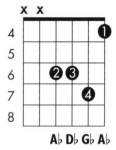

A♭ D♭ G♭ A♭

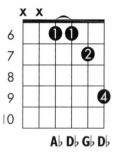

A♭ D♭ G♭ D♭

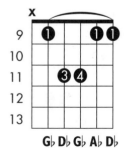

G♭ D♭ G♭ A♭ D♭

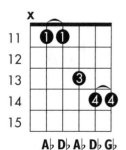

A♭ D♭ A♭ D♭ G♭

D♭5

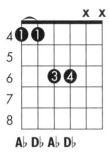

A♭ D♭ A♭ D♭

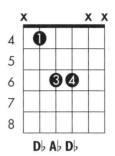

D♭ A♭ D♭

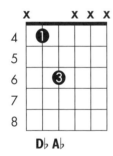

D♭ A♭

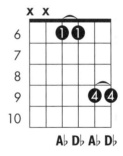

A♭ D♭ A♭ D♭

D♭

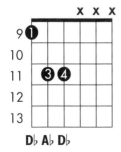

D♭ A♭ D♭

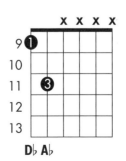

D♭ A♭

D♭6

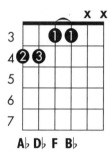

A♭ D♭ F B♭

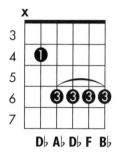

D♭ A♭ D♭ F B♭

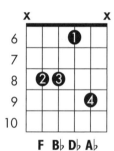

F B♭ D♭ A♭

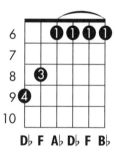

D♭ F A♭ D♭ F B♭

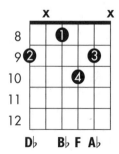

D♭ B♭ F A♭

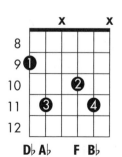

D♭ A♭ F B♭

D♭

D♭m6

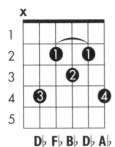

D♭ F♭ B♭ D♭ A♭

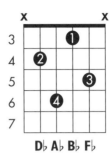

D♭ A♭ B♭ F♭

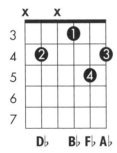

D♭ B♭ F♭ A♭

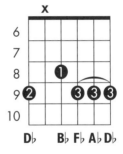

D♭ B♭ F♭ A♭ D♭

D♭

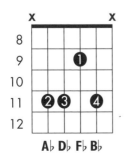

A♭ D♭ F♭ B♭

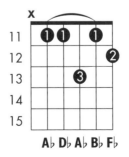

A♭ D♭ A♭ B♭ F♭

D♭7

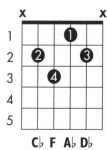

C♭ F A♭ D♭

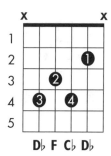

D♭ F C♭ D♭

D♭

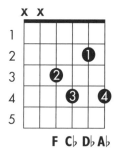

F C♭ D♭ A♭

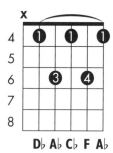

D♭ A♭ C♭ F A♭

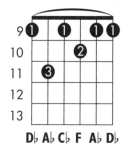

D♭ A♭ C♭ F A♭ D♭

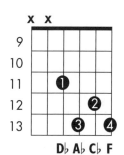

D♭ A♭ C♭ F

D♭maj7

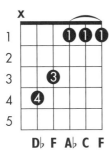

D♭ F A♭ C F

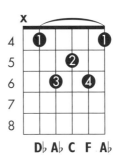

D♭ A♭ C F A♭

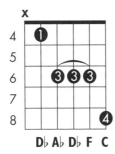

D♭ A♭ D♭ F C

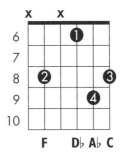

F   D♭ A♭ C

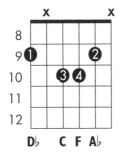

D♭   C F A♭

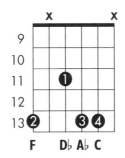

F   D♭ A♭ C

D♭m7

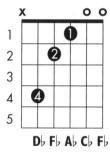

D♭ F♭ A♭ C♭ F♭

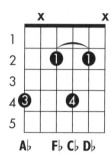

A♭　F♭ C♭ D♭

D♭

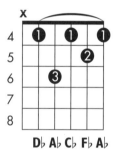

D♭ A♭ C♭ F♭ A♭

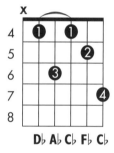

D♭ A♭ C♭ F♭ C♭

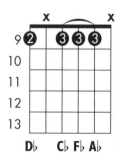

D♭　C♭ F♭ A♭

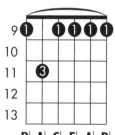

D♭ A♭ C♭ F♭ A♭ D♭

D♭m7(♭5)

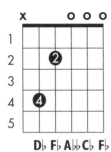

D♭ F♭ A♭♭ C♭ F♭

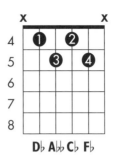

D♭ A♭♭ C♭ F♭

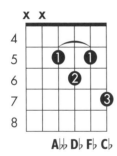

A♭♭ D♭ F♭ C♭

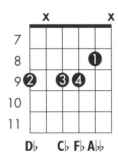

D♭　C♭ F♭ A♭♭

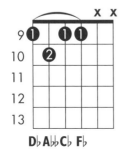

D♭ A♭♭ C♭ F♭

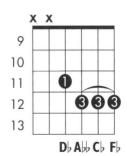

D♭ A♭♭ C♭ F♭

D♭

D♭°7

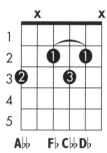

A♭♭ F♭ C♭♭ D♭

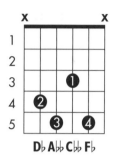

D♭ A♭♭ C♭♭ F♭

D♭

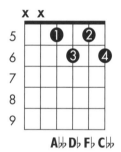

A♭♭ D♭ F♭ C♭♭

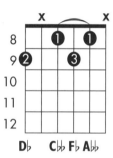

D♭ C♭♭ F♭ A♭♭

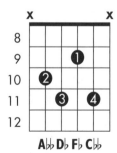

A♭♭ D♭ F♭ C♭♭

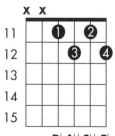

D♭ A♭♭ C♭♭ F♭

D♭9

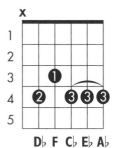

D♭ F C♭ E♭ A♭

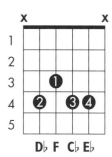

D♭ F C♭ E♭

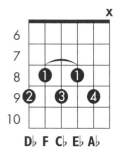

D♭ F C♭ E♭ A♭

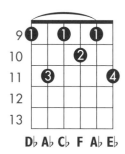

D♭ A♭ C♭ F A♭ E♭

D♭

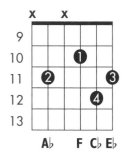

A♭ F C♭ E♭

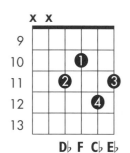

D♭ F C♭ E♭

D♭maj9

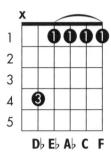

D♭ E♭ A♭ C F

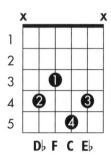

D♭ F C E♭

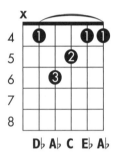

D♭ A♭ C E♭ A♭

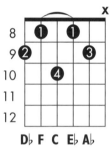

D♭ F C E♭ A♭

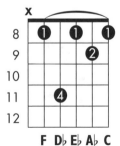

F D♭ E♭ A♭ C

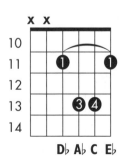

D♭ A♭ C E♭

D♭m9

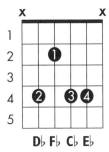

D♭ F♭ C♭ E♭

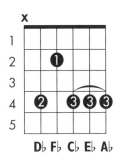

D♭ F♭ C♭ E♭ A♭

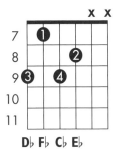

D♭ F♭ C♭ E♭

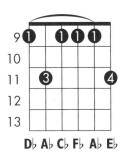

D♭ A♭ C♭ F♭ A♭ E♭

D♭

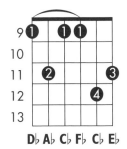

D♭ A♭ C♭ F♭ C♭ E♭

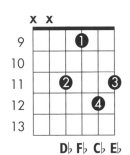

D♭ F♭ C♭ E♭

113

Dbmaj7(b5)

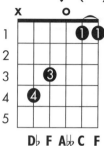

Db F Abb C F

Db7(b5)

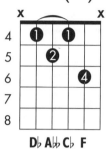

Db Abb Cb F

Db7+

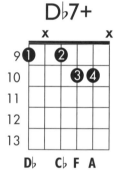

Db Cb F A

Db7(b9)

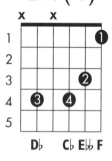

Db Cb Ebb F

Db7(#9)

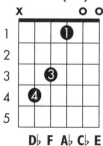

Db F Ab Cb E

Db9(b5)

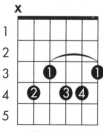

Db F Cb Eb Abb

Db

D

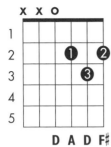

D A D F#

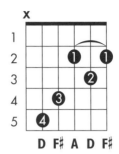

D F# A D F#

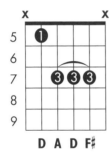

D A D F#

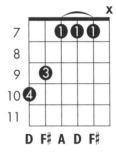

D F# A D F#

D

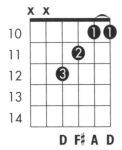

D F# A D

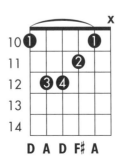

D A D F# A

Dm

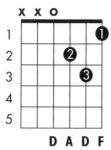

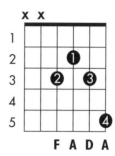

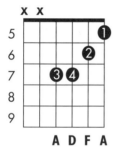

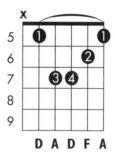

D

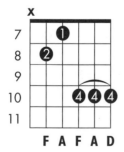

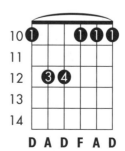

116

D+

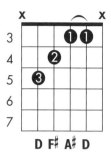

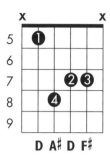

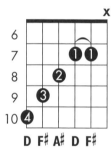

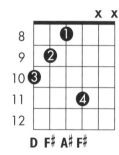

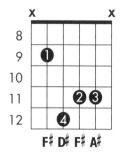

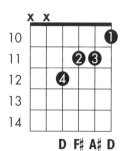

D

Dsus4

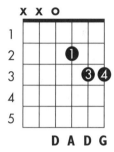

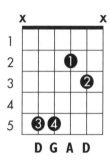

D

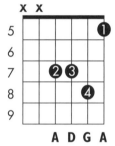

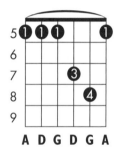

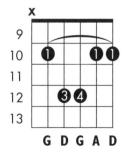

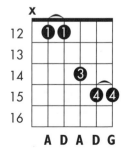

D5

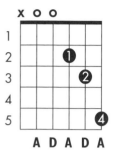

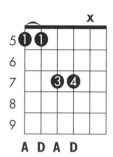

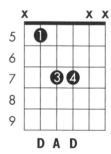

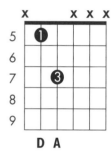

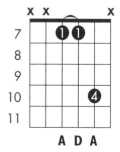

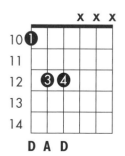

D

119

D6

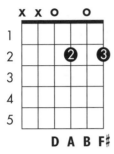

D A B F#

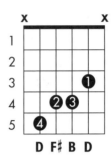

D F# B D

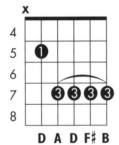

D A D F# B

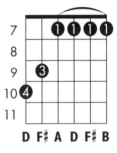

D F# A D F# B

D

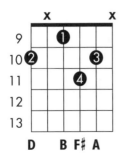

D B F# A

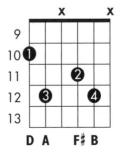

D A F# B

Dm6

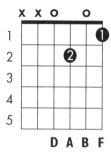

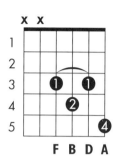

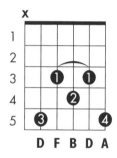

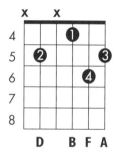

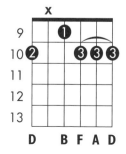

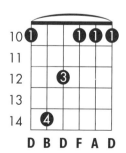

D

D7

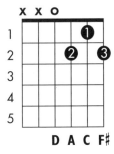

D A C F#

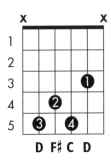

D F# C D

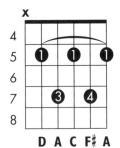

D A C F# A

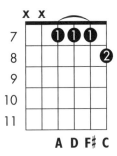

A D F# C

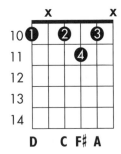

D C F# A

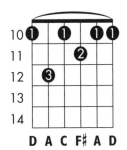

D A C F# A D

D

Dmaj7

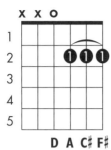

D A C# F#

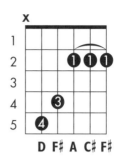

D F# A C# F#

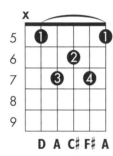

D A C# F# A

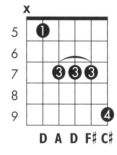

D A D F# C#

D

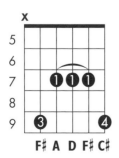

F# A D F# C#

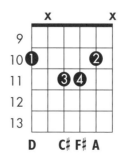

D C# F# A

Dm7

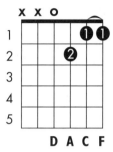

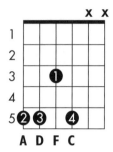

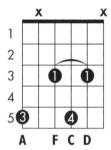

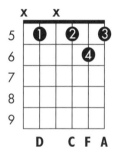

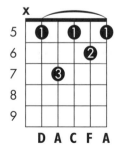

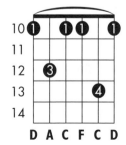

D

Dm7($\flat$5)

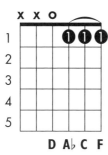

D A$\flat$ C F

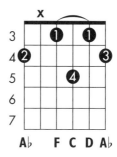

A$\flat$ F C D A$\flat$

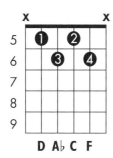

D A$\flat$ C F

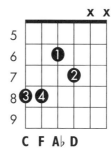

C F A$\flat$ D

D

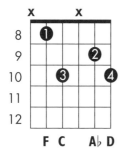

F C A$\flat$ D

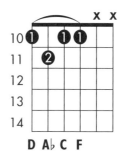

D A$\flat$ C F

D°7

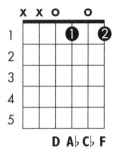

D A♭ C♭ F

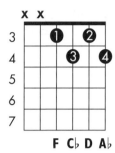

F C♭ D A♭

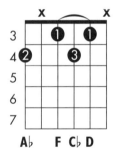

A♭ F C♭ D

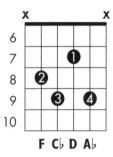

F C♭ D A♭

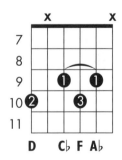

D C♭ F A♭

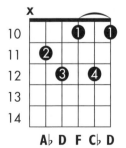

A♭ D F C♭ D

D

D9

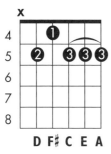

D F# C E A

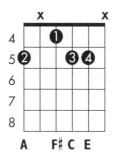

A F# C E

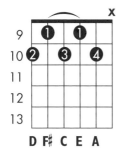

D F# C E A

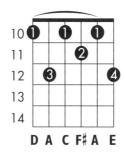

D A C F# A E

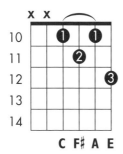

C F# A E

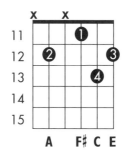

A F# C E

D

Dmaj9

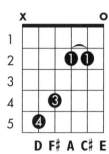

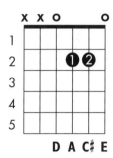

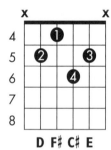

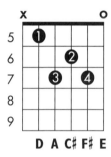

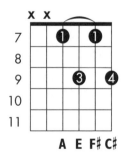

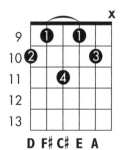

Dm9

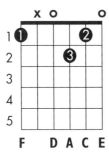

F D A C E

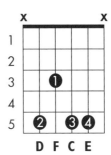

D F C E

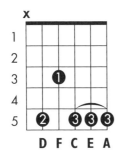

D F C E A

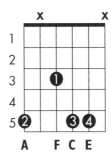

A F C E

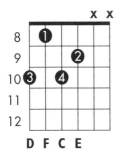

D F C E

D A C F A E

D

Dmaj7(♭5)

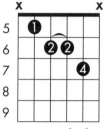

D A♭ C♯ F♯

D7(♭5)

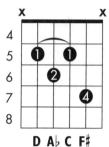

D A♭ C F♯

D7+

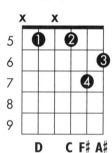

D   C F♯ A♯

D7(♭9)

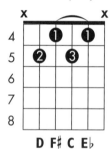

D F♯ C E♭

D7(♯9)

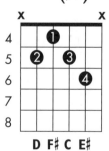

D F♯ C E♯

D9(♭5)

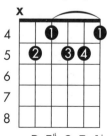

D F♯ C E A♭

D

E♭

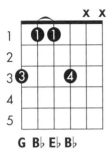

G B♭ E♭ B♭

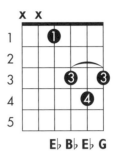

E♭ B♭ E♭ G

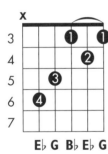

E♭ G B♭ E♭ G

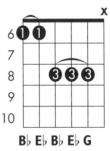

B♭ E♭ B♭ E♭ G

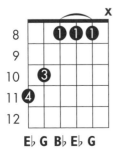

E♭ G B♭ E♭ G

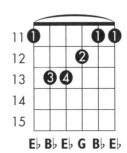

E♭ B♭ E♭ G B♭ E♭

E♭

131

E♭m

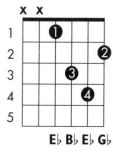

E♭ B♭ E♭ G♭

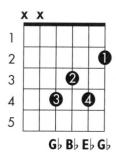

G♭ B♭ E♭ G♭

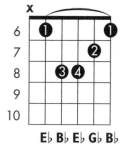

E♭ B♭ E♭ G♭ B♭

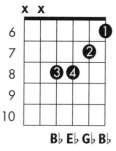

B♭ E♭ G♭ B♭

E♭

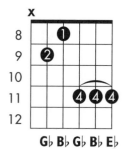

G♭ B♭ G♭ B♭ E♭

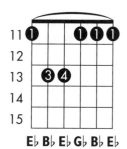

E♭ B♭ E♭ G♭ B♭ E♭

E♭+

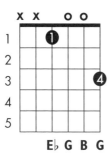

E♭ G B G

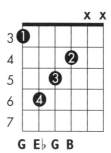

G E♭ G B

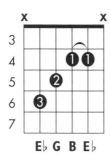

E♭ G B E♭

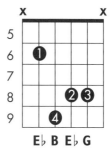

E♭ B E♭ G

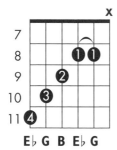

E♭ G B E♭ G

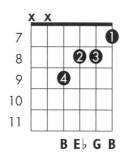

B E♭ G B

E♭

E♭sus4

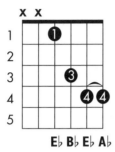

E♭ B♭ E♭ A♭

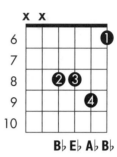

B♭ E♭ A♭ B♭

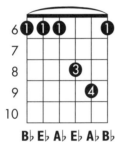

B♭ E♭ A♭ E♭ A♭ B♭

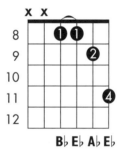

B♭ E♭ A♭ E♭

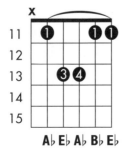

A♭ E♭ A♭ B♭ E♭

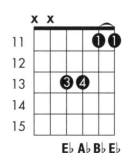

E♭ A♭ B♭ E♭

E♭

E♭5

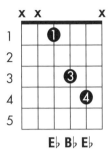

E♭ B♭ E♭

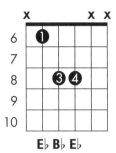

E♭ B♭ E♭

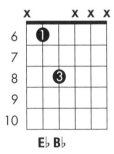

E♭ B♭

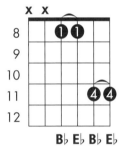

B♭ E♭ B♭ E♭

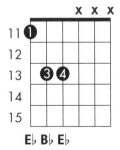

E♭ B♭ E♭

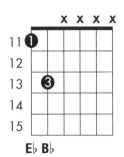

E♭ B♭

E♭

E♭6

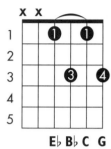

E♭ B♭ C G

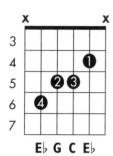

E♭ G C E♭

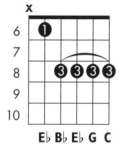

E♭ B♭ E♭ G C

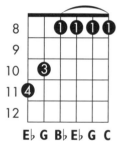

E♭ G B♭ E♭ G C

E♭

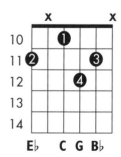

E♭ C G B♭

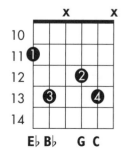

E♭ B♭ G C

E♭m6

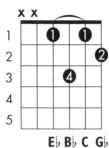

E♭ B♭ C G♭

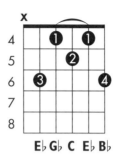

E♭ G♭ C E♭ B♭

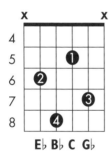

E♭ B♭ C G♭

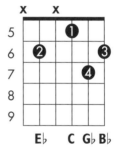

E♭ C G♭ B♭

E♭

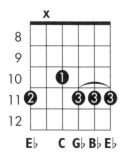

E♭ C G♭ B♭ E♭

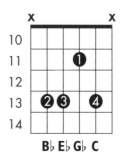

B♭ E♭ G♭ C

E♭7

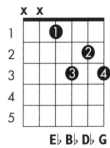

E♭ B♭ D♭ G

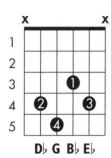

D♭ G B♭ E♭

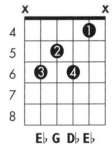

E♭ G D♭ E♭

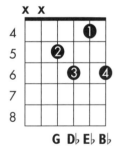

G D♭ E♭ B♭

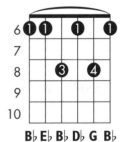

B♭ E♭ B♭ D♭ G B♭

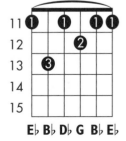

E♭ B♭ D♭ G B♭ E♭

E♭

E♭maj7

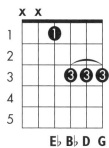

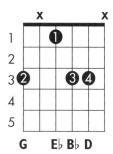

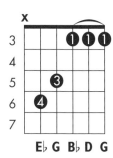

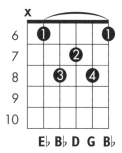

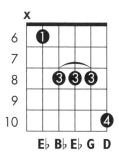

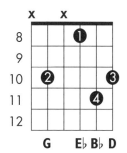

E♭

E♭m7

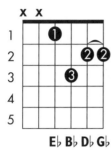

E♭ B♭ D♭ G♭

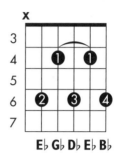

E♭ G♭ D♭ E♭ B♭

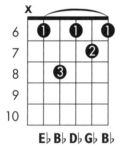

E♭ B♭ D♭ G♭ B♭

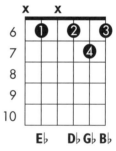

E♭   D♭ G♭ B♭

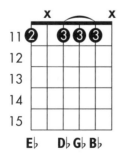

E♭   D♭ G♭ B♭

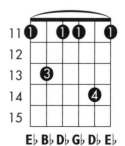

E♭ B♭ D♭ G♭ D♭ E♭

E♭

E♭m7(♭5)

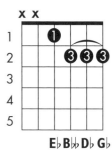

E♭ B♭♭ D♭ G♭

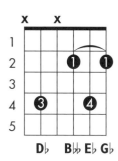

D♭ B♭♭ E♭ G♭

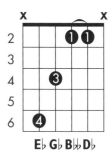

E♭ G♭ B♭♭ D♭

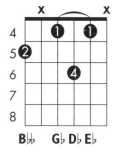

B♭♭ G♭ D♭ E♭

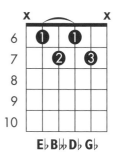

E♭ B♭♭ D♭ G♭

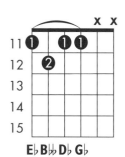

E♭ B♭♭ D♭ G♭

E♭

E♭°7

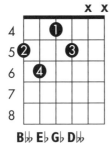

G♭   E♭ B♭♭ D♭♭

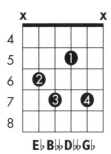

E♭ B♭♭ D♭♭ G♭

B♭♭ E♭ G♭ D♭♭

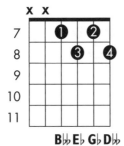

E♭ B♭♭ D♭♭ G♭

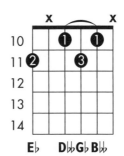

B♭♭ E♭ G♭ D♭♭

E♭   D♭♭ G♭ B♭♭

E♭

E♭9

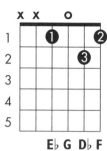

E♭ G D♭ F

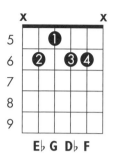

E♭ G D♭ F

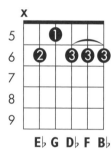

E♭ G D♭ F B♭

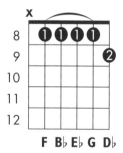

F B♭ E♭ G D♭

E♭

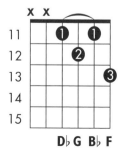

D♭ G B♭ F

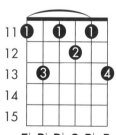

E♭ B♭ D♭ G B♭ F

E♭maj9

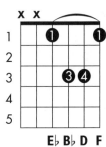

E♭ B♭ D F

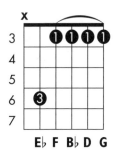

E♭ F B♭ D G

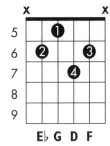

E♭ G D F

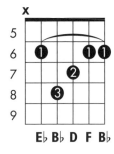

E♭ B♭ D F B♭

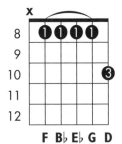

F B♭ E♭ G D

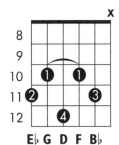

E♭ G D F B♭

E♭

E♭m9

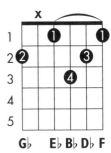

G♭   E♭ B♭ D♭ F

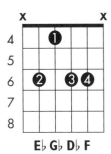

E♭ G♭ D♭ F

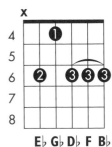

E♭ G♭ D♭ F B♭

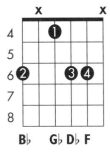

B♭   G♭ D♭ F

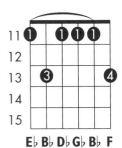

E♭ B♭ D♭ G♭ B♭ F

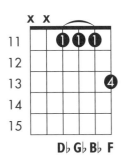

D♭ G♭ B♭ F

E♭

E♭maj7(♭5)

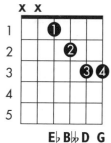

E♭ B♭♭ D G

E♭7(♭5)

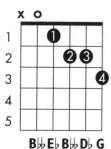

B♭♭ E♭ B♭♭ D♭ G

E♭7+

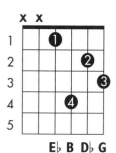

E♭ B D♭ G

E♭7(♭9)

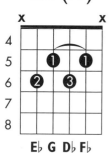

E♭ G D♭ F♭

E♭7(♯9)

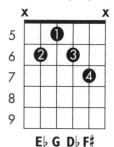

E♭ G D♭ F♯

E♭9(♭5)

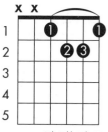

E♭ B♭♭ D♭ F

E♭

E

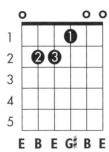

E B E G♯ B E

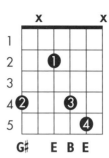

G♯ E B E

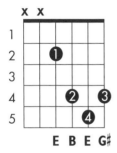

E B E G♯

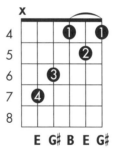

E G♯ B E G♯

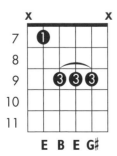

E B E G♯

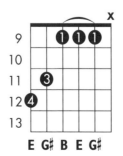

E G♯ B E G♯

E

147

Em

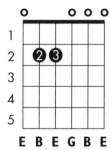

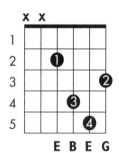

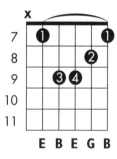

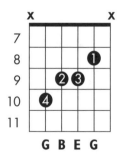

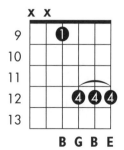

E+

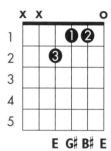

E G# B# E

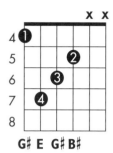

G# E G# B#

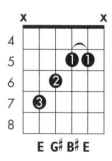

E G# B# E

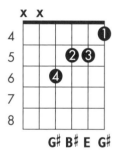

G# B# E G#

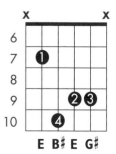

E B# E G#

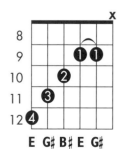

E G# B# E G#

E

Esus4

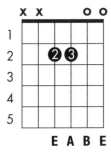

E A B E

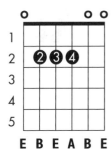

E B E A B E

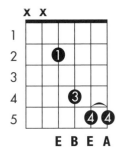

E B E A

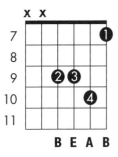

B E A B

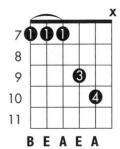

B E A E A

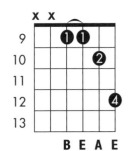

B E A E

E5

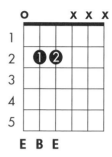

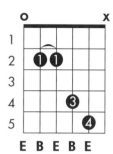

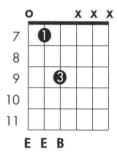

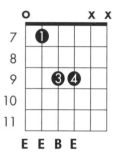

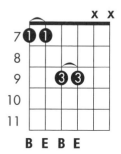

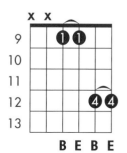

E

151

E6

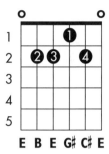

E B E G# C# E

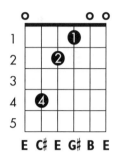

E C# E G# B E

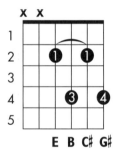

E B C# G#

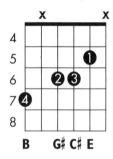

B   G# C# E

E

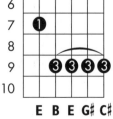

E B E G# C#

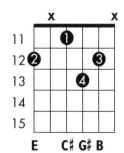

E   C# G# B

Em6

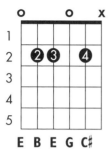

E B E G C#

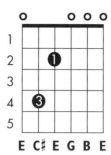

E C# E G B E

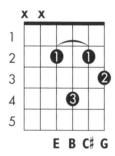

E B C# G

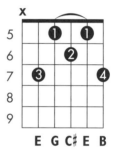

E G C# E B

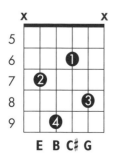

E B C# G

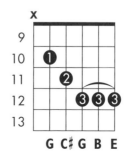

G C# G B E

E

153

E7

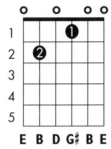

E B D G# B E

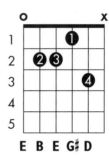

E B E G# D

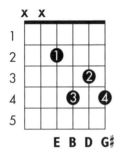

E B D G#

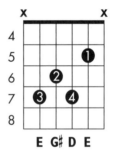

E G# D E

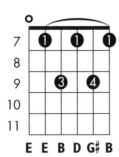

E E B D G# B

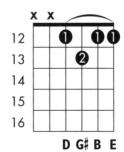

D G# B E

E

Emaj7

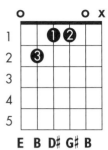

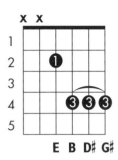

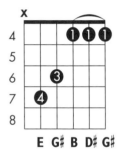

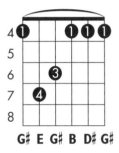

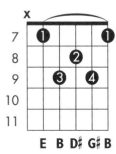

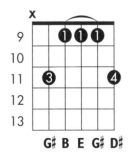

Em7

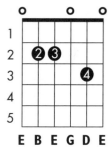

E B E G D E

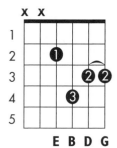

E B D G B E

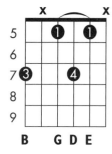

E B D G

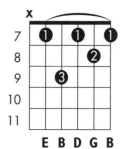

B G D E

E

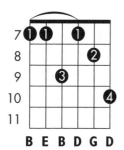

E B D G B

B E B D G D

Em7(♭5)

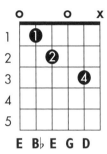

E B♭ E G D

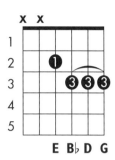

E B♭ D G

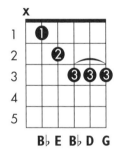

B♭ E B♭ D G

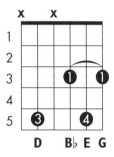

D B♭ E G

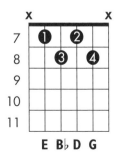

E B♭ D G

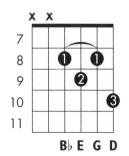

B♭ E G D

E

157

E°7

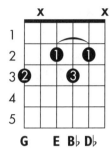

G   E B♭ D♭

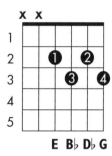

E B♭ D♭ G

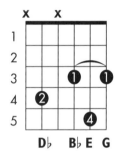

D♭   B♭ E G

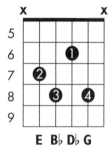

E B♭ D♭ G

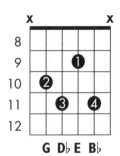

G D♭ E B♭

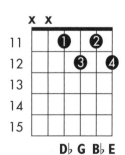

D♭ G B♭ E

E

E9

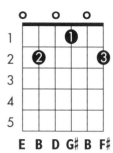

E B D G# B F#

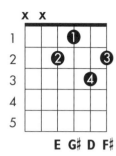

E G# D F#

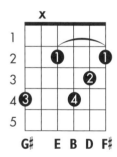

G# E B D F#

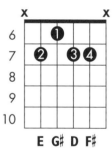

E G# D F#

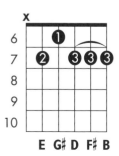

E G# D F# B

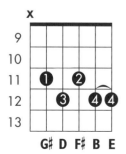

G# D F# B E

Emaj9

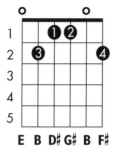

E B D# G# B F#

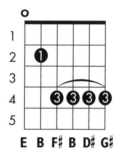

E B F# B D# G#

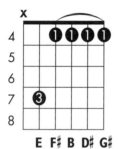

E F# B D# G#

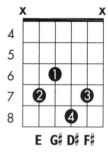

E G# D# F#

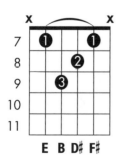

E B D# F#

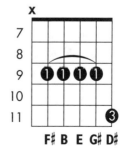

F# B E G# D#

E

Em9

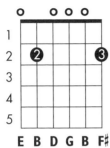

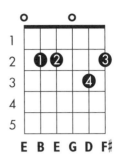

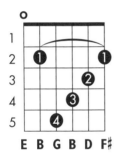

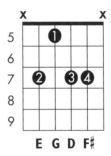

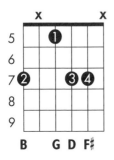

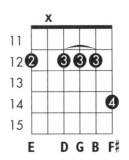

E

Emaj7(♭5)

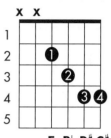

x x

E B♭ D♯ G♯

E7(♭5)

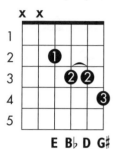

x x

E B♭ D G♯

E7+

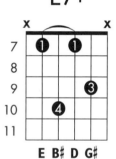

x x

E B♯ D G♯

E7(♭9)

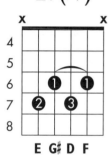

x x

E G♯ D F

E7(♯9)

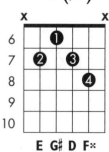

x x

E G♯ D F⁑

E9(♭5)

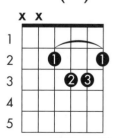

x x

E B♭ D F♯

E

F

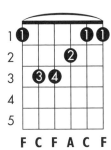

F C F A C F

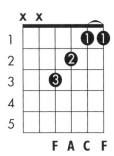

F A C F

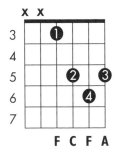

F C F A

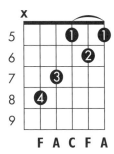

F A C F A

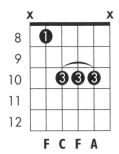

F C F A

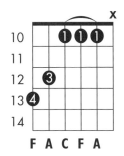

F A C F A

F

Fm

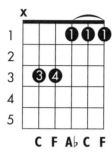

C F A♭ C F

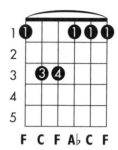

F C F A♭ C F

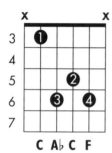

C A♭ C F

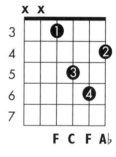

F C F A♭

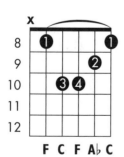

F C F A♭ C

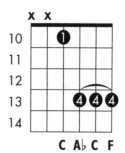

C A♭ C F

F

F+

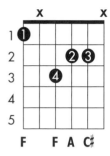

F   F A C♯

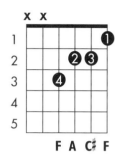

F A C♯ F

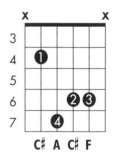

C♯ A C♯ F

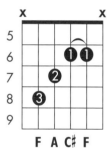

F A C♯ F

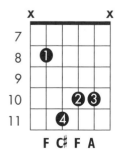

F C♯ F A

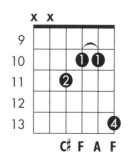

C♯ F A F

F

165

Fsus4

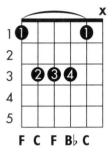

F C F B♭ C

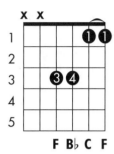

F B♭ C F

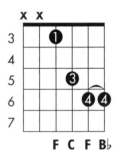

F C F B♭

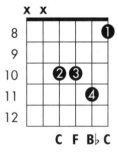

C F B♭ C

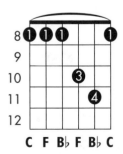

C F B♭ F B♭ C

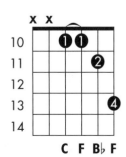

C F B♭ F

F

F5

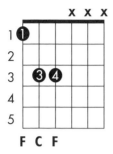

F C F

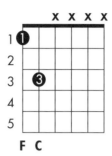

F C

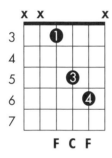

F C F

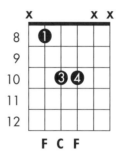

F C F

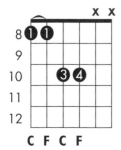

C F C F

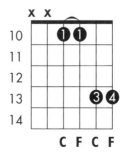

C F C F

F

F6

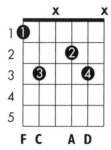

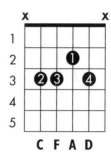

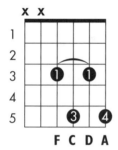

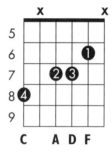

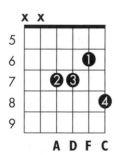

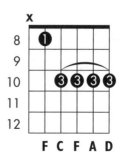

F

Fm6

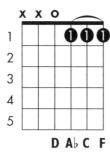

D A♭ C F

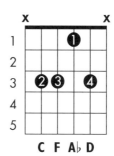

C F A♭ D

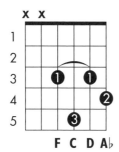

F C D A♭

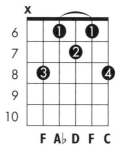

F A♭ D F C

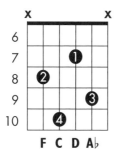

F C D A♭

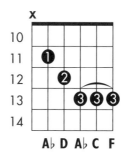

A♭ D A♭ C F

F

F7

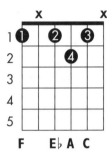

F   E♭ A C

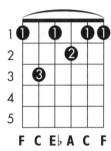

F C E♭ A C F

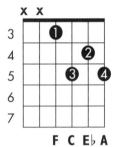

F C E♭ A

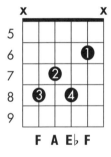

F A E♭ F

F

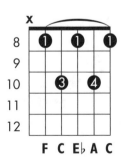

F C E♭ A C

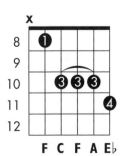

F C F A E♭

Fmaj7

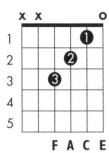

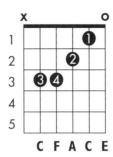

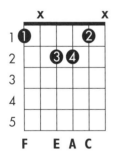

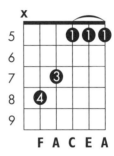

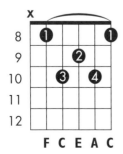

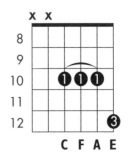

F

Fm7

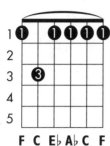

F C E♭ A♭ C F

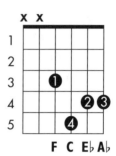

F C E♭ A♭

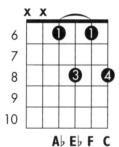

A♭ E♭ F C

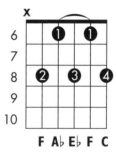

F A♭ E♭ F C

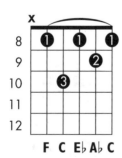

F C E♭ A♭ C

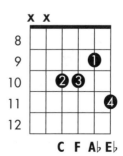

C F A♭ E♭

F

Fm7(♭5)

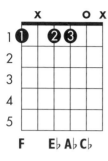

F   E♭ A♭ C♭

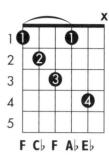

F C♭ F A♭ E♭

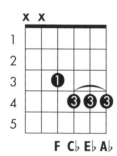

F C♭ E♭ A♭

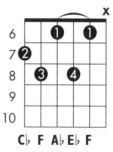

C♭ F A♭ E♭ F

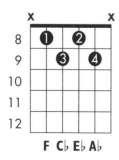

F C♭ E♭ A♭

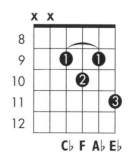

C♭ F A♭ E♭

F

F°7

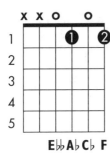

E♭♭ A♭ C♭ F

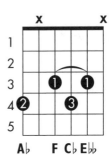

A♭　F C♭ E♭♭

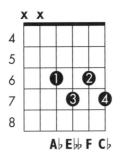

A♭ E♭♭ F C♭

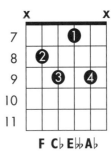

F C♭ E♭♭ A♭

F

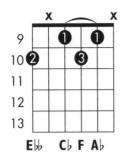

E♭♭　C♭ F A♭

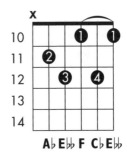

A♭ E♭♭ F C♭ E♭♭

F9

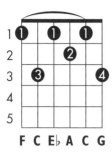

F C E♭ A C G

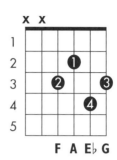

F A E♭ G

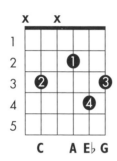

C A E♭ G

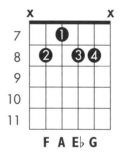

F A E♭ G

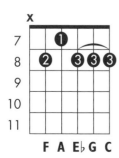

F A E♭ G C

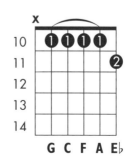

G C F A E♭

F

175

Fmaj9

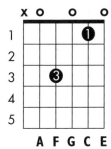

A F G C E

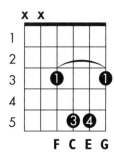

F C E G

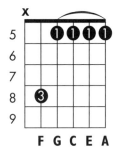

F G C E A

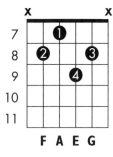

F A E G

F

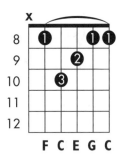

F C E G C

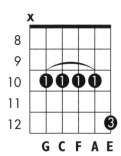

G C F A E

Fm9

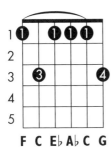

F C E♭ A♭ C G

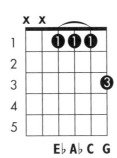

E♭ A♭ C G

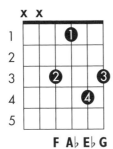

F A♭ E♭ G

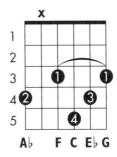

A♭ F C E♭ G

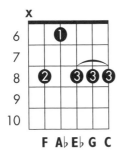

F A♭ E♭ G C

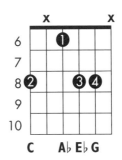

C A♭ E♭ G

F

177

Fmaj7(♭5)

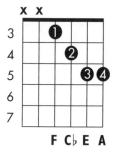

F C♭ E A

F7(♭5)

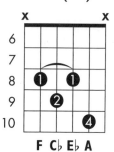

F C♭ E♭ A

F7+

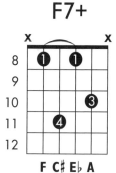

F C# E♭ A

F7(♭9)

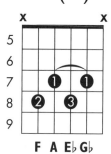

F A E♭ G♭

F7(#9)

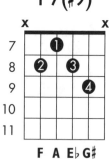

F A E♭ G#

F9(♭5)

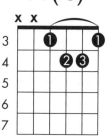

F C♭ E♭ G

F

178

F#

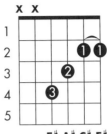

x
1
2 ❶❶
3   ❷
4 ❸❹
5
C# F# A# C# F#

x x
1
2 ❶❶
3   ❷
4 ❸
5
F# A# C# F#

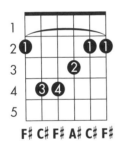

1
2 ❶   ❶❶
3   ❷
4 ❸❹
5
F# C# F# A# C# F#

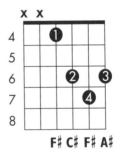

x x
4 ❶
5
6   ❷ ❸
7   ❹
8
F# C# F# A#

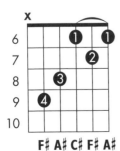

x
6 ❶ ❶
7   ❷
8 ❸
9 ❹
10
F# A# C# F# A#

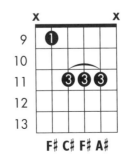

x   x
9 ❶
10
11 ❸❸❸
12
13
F# C# F# A#

F#

179

F#m

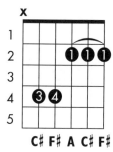

C# F# A C# F#

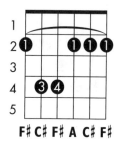

F# C# F# A C# F#

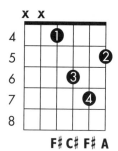

F# C# F# A

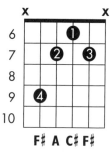

F# A C# F#

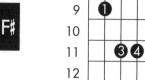

F# C# F# A C#

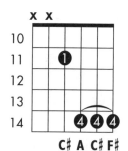

C# A C# F#

F#

F#+

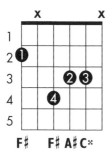

F#   F# A# Cx

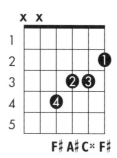

F# A# Cx F#

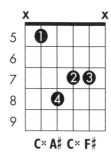

Cx A# Cx F#

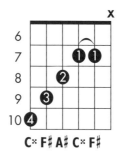

Cx F# A# Cx F#

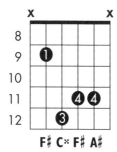

F# Cx F# A#

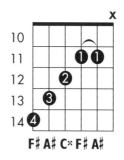

F# A# Cx F# A#

F#

181

F#sus4

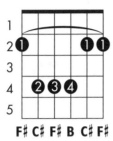

F# C# F# B C# F#

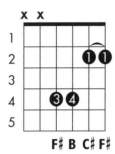

F# B C# F#

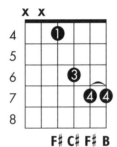

F# C# F# B

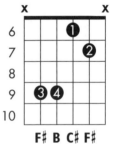

F# B C# F#

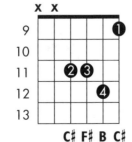

C# F# B C#

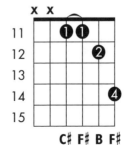

C# F# B F#

F#

F#5

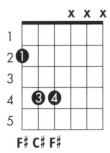

F# C# F#

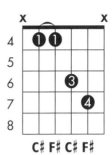

C# F# C# F#

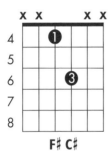

F# C#

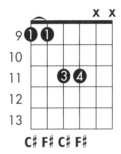

C# F# C# F#

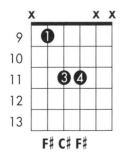

F# C# F#

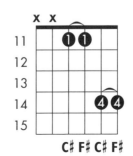

C# F# C# F#

F#

F#6

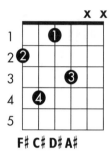

F# C# D# A#

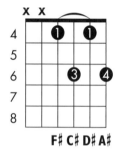

F#   D# A# C#

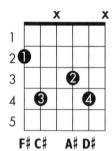

F# C#   A# D#

X X

4
5
6
7
8

F# C# D# A#

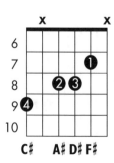

C#   A# D# F#

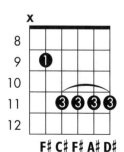

F# C# F# A# D#

F#m6

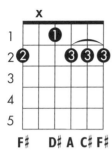

F# D# A C# F#

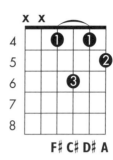

F# C# D# A

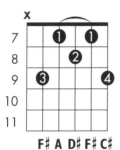

F# A D# F# C#

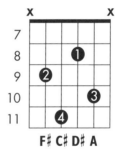

F# C# D# A

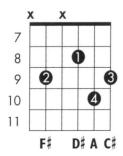

F# D# A C#

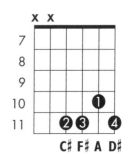

C# F# A D#

F#

F#7

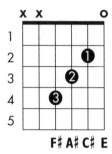

F# A# C# E

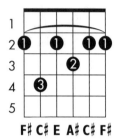

F# C# E A# C# F#

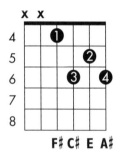

F# C# E A#

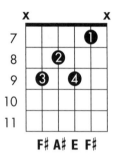

F# A# E F#

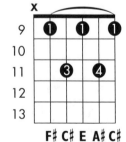

F# C# E A# C#

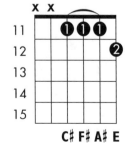

C# F# A# E

F#

F#maj7

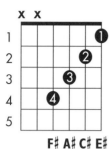

F# A# C# E#

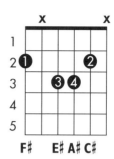

F# E# A# C#

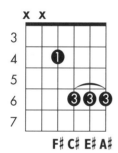

F# C# E# A#

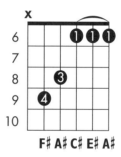

F# A# C# E# A#

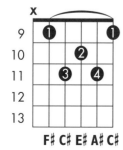

F# C# E# A# C#

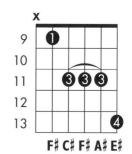

F# C# F# A# E#

F#

F#m7

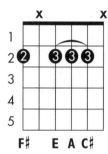

F# E A C#

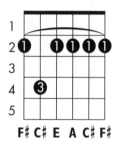

F# C# E A C# F#

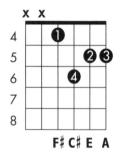

F# C# E A

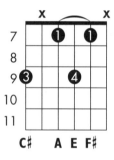

C# A E F#

F#

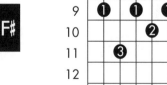

F# C# E A C#

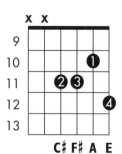

C# F# A E

F#m7(♭5)

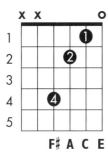

F# A C E

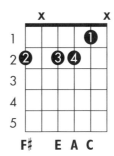

F# E A C

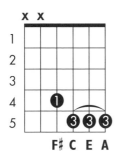

F# C E A

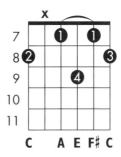

C A E F# C

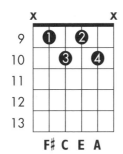

F# C E A

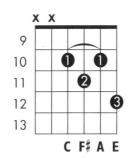

C F# A E

F#

F#°7

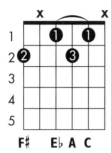

F# Eb A C

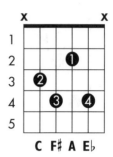

C F# A Eb

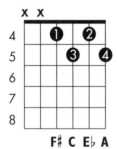

F# C Eb A

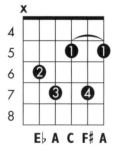

Eb A C F# A

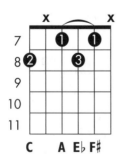

C A Eb F#

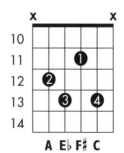

A Eb F# C

F#

F#9

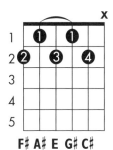

F# A# E G# C#

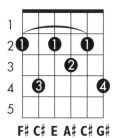

F# C# E A# C# G#

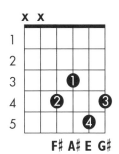

F# A# E G#

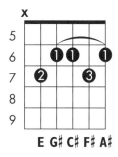

E G# C# F# A#

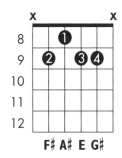

F# A# E G#

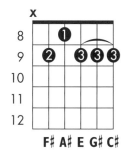

F# A# E G# C#

F#

191

F#maj9

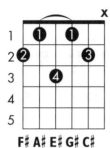

F# A# E# G# C#

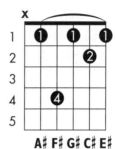

A# F# G# C# E#

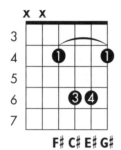

F# C# E# G#

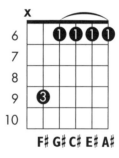

F# G# C# E# A#

F#

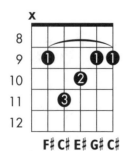

F# C# E# G# C#

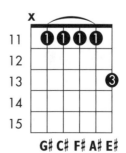

G# C# F# A# E#

F#m9

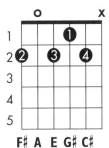

F# A E G# C#

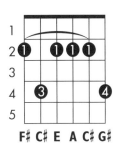

F# C# E A C# G#

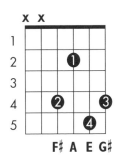

F# A E G#

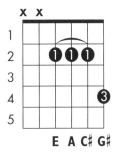

E A C# G#

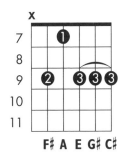

F# A E G# C#

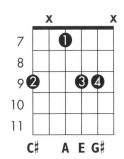

C# A E G#

F#

F#maj7(♭5)

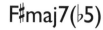
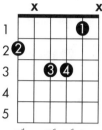

x · · · x

1 · · · ❶
2 ❷ · · ·
3 · · ❸ ❹
4 · · · ·
5 · · · ·

F#　E#　A#C

F#7(♭5)

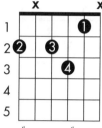

x · · · x

1 · · · ❶
2 ❷ · ❸ ·
3 · · · ❹
4 · · · ·
5 · · · ·

F#　E　A#C

F#7+

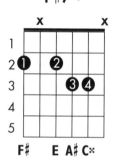

x · · · x

1 · · · ·
2 ❶ · ❷ ·
3 · · ❸ ❹
4 · · · ·
5 · · · ·

F#　E　A#C✳

F#7(♭9)

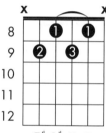

x · · · x

8 · ❶ · ❶
9 ❷ · ❸ ·
10 · · · ·
11 · · · ·
12 · · · ·

F#A#　E　G

F#7(#9)

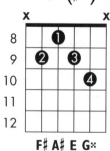

x · · · x

8 · ❶ · ·
9 ❷ · ❸ ·
10 · · · ❹
11 · · · ·
12 · · · ·

F#A#　E　G✳

F#9(♭5)

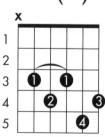

x · · · ·

1 · · · ·
2 · · · ·
3 ❶ · ❶ ·
4 · ❷ · ❸
5 · · ❹ ·

C　F#A#　E　G#

F#

G

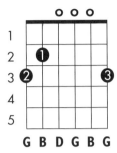

G B D G B G

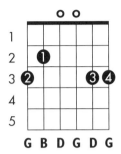

G B D G D G

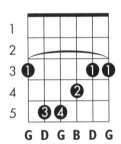

G D G B D G

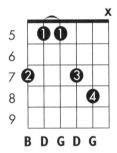

B D G D G

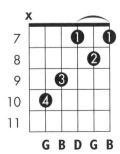

G B D G B

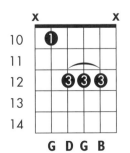

G D G B

G

195

Gm

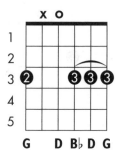

G   D   Bb D   G

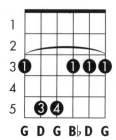

G D G Bb D G

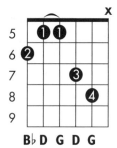

Bb D   G   D   G

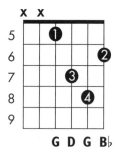

G D G Bb

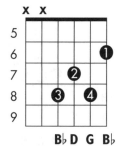

Bb D   G   Bb

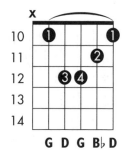

G D G Bb D

G+

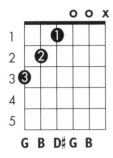

G B D# G B

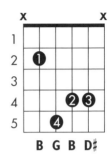

B G B D#

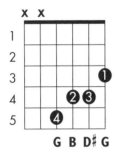

G B D# G

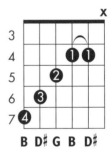

B D# G B D#

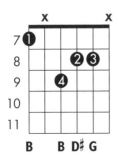

B B D# G

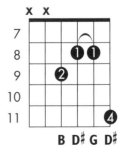

B D# G D#

G

Gsus4

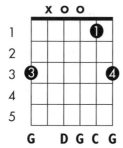

G　　D G C G

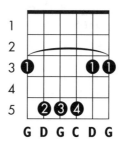

G D G C D G

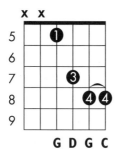

G D G C

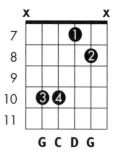

G C D G

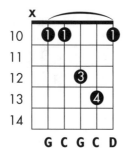

G C G C D

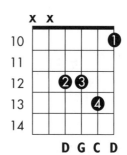

D G C D

G

G5

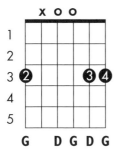

G   D G D G

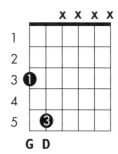

G D

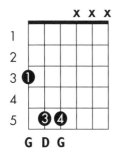

G D G

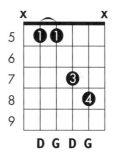

D G D G

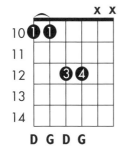

D G D G

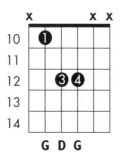

G D G

G

199

G6

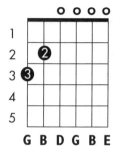

G B D G B E

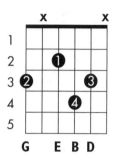

G E B D

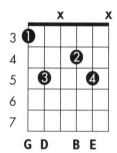

G D B E

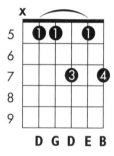

D G D E B

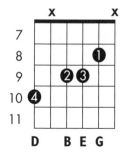

D B E G

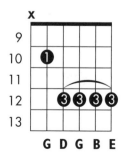

G D G B E

Gm6

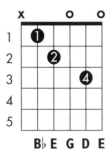

Bb E G D E

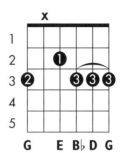

G   E Bb D G

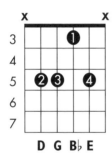

D G Bb E

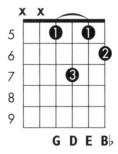

G D E Bb

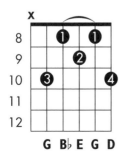

G Bb E G D

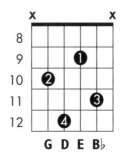

G D E Bb

G

G7

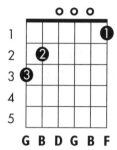

G B D G B F

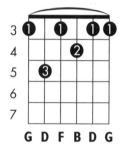

G D F B D G

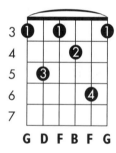

G D F B F G

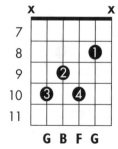

G B F G

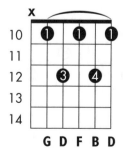

G D F B D

G

Gmaj7

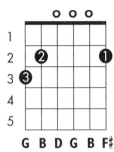

G B D G B F#

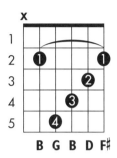

B G B D F#

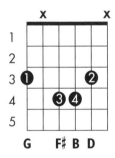

G F# B D

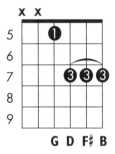

G D F# B

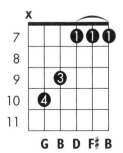

G B D F# B

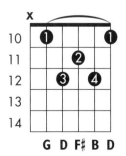

G D F# B D

G

Gm7

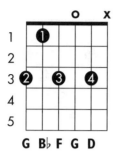

G B♭ F G D

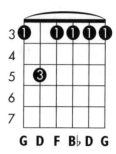

G D F B♭ D G

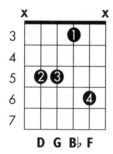

D G B♭ F

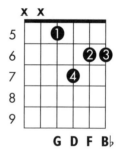

G D F B♭

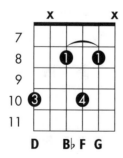

D B♭ F G

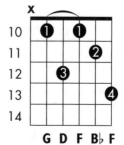

G D F B♭ F

G

Gm7(♭5)

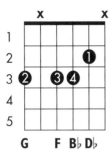

G   F B♭ D♭

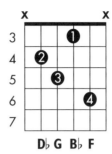

D♭ G B♭ F

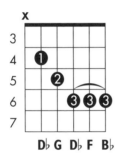

D♭ G D♭ F B♭

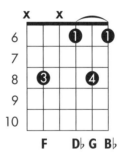

F   D♭ G B♭

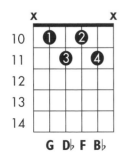

G D♭ F B♭

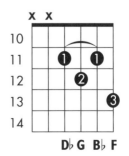

D♭ G B♭ F

G

205

G°7

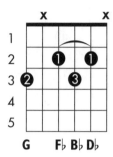

G F♭ B♭ D♭

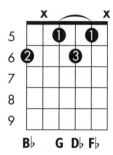

B♭ G D♭ F♭

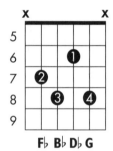

F♭ B♭ D♭ G

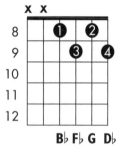

B♭ F♭ G D♭

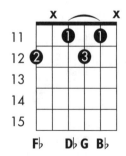

F♭ D♭ G B♭

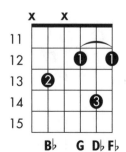

B♭ G D♭ F♭

G

G9

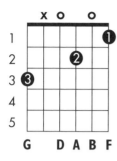

G D A B F

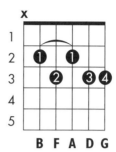

B F A D G

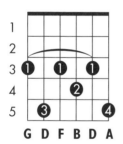

G D F B D A

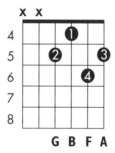

G B F A

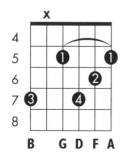

B G D F A

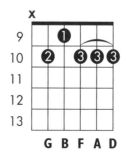

G B F A D

G

207

Gmaj9

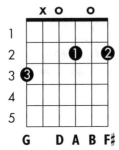

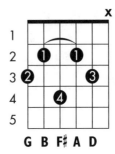

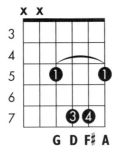

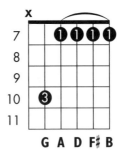

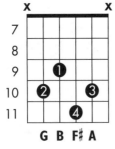

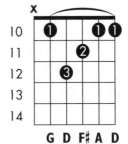

G

Gm9

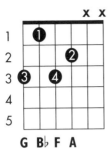

G B♭ F A

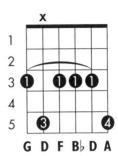

G D F B♭ D A

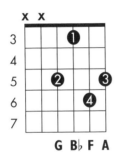

G B♭ F A

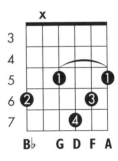

B♭ G D F A

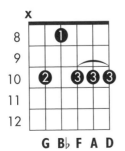

G B♭ F A D

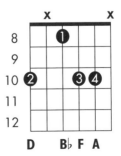

D B♭ F A

G

Gmaj7(♭5)

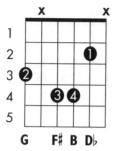

G7(♭5)

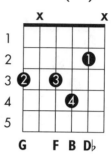

G7+

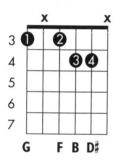

G7(♭9)

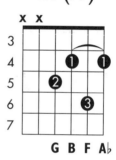

G7(♯9)

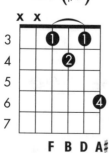

G9(♭5)

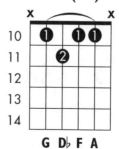

G

Moveable Barre Chords

Definitions

The chords in this section are called "moveable" because once a single fingering formation is learned, it can be moved up and down the fingerboard. In this way, a single fingering can be used for as many as 12 different chords.

A *barre* means to hold down two or more strings using only one finger. If the finger holds down all six strings, the barre is called "full."

How to Form Barre Chords

To form any barre chord, proceed in this manner:

1. Select an open-string chord, in this example, E major.

2. Alter the fingering so that the 1st finger is free.

3. Slide the fingers one fret up the fingerboard, and, without moving the other fingers, place the 1st finger straight across the 1st fret and press firmly.

The chord you are now playing is a moveable barre chord. This chord can be moved to any fret on the guitar (up to about the 12th fret on most models).

Roots and Barre Chords

Remember, every chord has a *root*. The root is the note that names the chord. For example, the root of an E major chord is the note E; the root of an A minor chord is the note A; the root of a C7 chord is the note C, and so on.

When using barre chords, it is important to remember that, regardless of the fret on which the barre chord is played, the root always remains on the same string.

In the example on the previous page, the root of the E major chord was the note E. This note is found on the open 6th string.

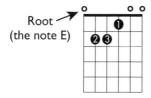

After moving the chord up one fret, the root remains on the 6th string.

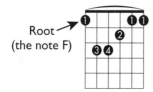

Since the name of this note is F and since we started with a major chord form, the name of this chord is F major. If we move the chord up one more fret, the root is found on the 6th string at the 2nd fret.

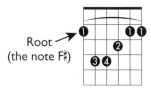

Root → (the note F♯)

The name of this note is F♯ (or G♭). Therefore, the chord is F♯ (or G♭) major. Similarly, with the barre across the 3rd fret, the chord is G major; across the 4th fret, G♯ or A♭ major; across the 5th fret, A major; and so on.

In the following pages, you will learn how to play nine different types of moveable chords, each of which has a fingering with the root on the 6th string and one with the root on the 5th string. So, in total, you will learn 18 different fingerings (9x2).

By applying the same method discussed on the previous two pages, you can play 12 different chords with each fingering. Multiply 12 by 18 (the total number of fingerings in this section), and you have 216—the number of chords you will be able to play by learning only 18 fingerings and the notes on the fingerboard.

NOTE: To review the notes on the fingerboard, you can refer to the illustration on page 232.

Moveable Major Chord
(With the Root on the 6th String)

Based on the Open E Chord

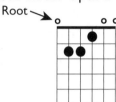

Root

Moveable Barre Form

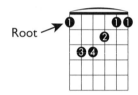

Root

With Root At:		
1st fret	=	F
2nd fret	=	F♯ (G♭)
3rd fret	=	G
4th fret	=	A♭ (G♯)
5th fret	=	A
6th fret	=	B♭ (A♯)
7th fret	=	B
8th fret	=	C
9th fret	=	D♭ (C♯)
10th fret	=	D
11th fret	=	E♭ (D♯)
12th fret	=	E

Moveable Major Chord
(With the Root on the 5th String)

Based on the Open A Chord

Root

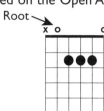

Moveable Barre Form

Root

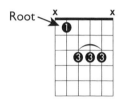

With Root At:

1st fret	=	B♭ (A♯)
2nd fret	=	B
3rd fret	=	C
4th fret	=	D♭ (C♯)
5th fret	=	D
6th fret	=	E♭ (D♯)
7th fret	=	E
8th fret	=	F
9th fret	=	F♯ (G♭)
10th fret	=	G
11th fret	=	A♭ (G♯)
12th fret	=	A

Moveable Minor Chord
(With the Root on the 6th String)

Based on the Open Em Chord

Root

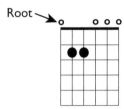

Moveable Barre Form

Root

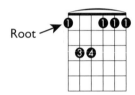

With Root At:

1st fret	=	Fm
2nd fret	=	F♯m (G♭m)
3rd fret	=	Gm
4th fret	=	A♭m (G♯m)
5th fret	=	Am
6th fret	=	B♭m (A♯m)
7th fret	=	Bm
8th fret	=	Cm
9th fret	=	D♭m (C♯m)
10th fret	=	Dm
11th fret	=	E♭m (D♯m)
12th fret	=	Em

Moveable Minor Chord
(With the Root on the 5th String)

Based on the Open Am Chord

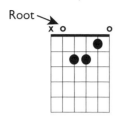

Moveable Barre Form

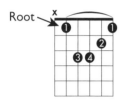

With Root At:

1st fret	=	B♭m (A♯m)
2nd fret	=	Bm
3rd fret	=	Cm
4th fret	=	D♭m (C♯m)
5th fret	=	Dm
6th fret	=	E♭m (D♯m)
7th fret	=	Em
8th fret	=	Fm
9th fret	=	F♯m (G♭m)
10th fret	=	Gm
11th fret	=	A♭m (G♯m)
12th fret	=	Am

Moveable 5th Chord
(With the Root on the 6th String)

Although this isn't a barre chord, it is an important and popular
moveable chord, so it is included in this section.

Based on the Open E5 Chord

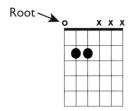

Root

Moveable Form

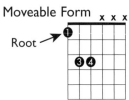

Root

With Root At:

1st fret	=	F5
2nd fret	=	F♯5 (G♭5)
3rd fret	=	G5
4th fret	=	A♭5 (G♯5)
5th fret	=	A5
6th fret	=	B♭5 (A♯5)
7th fret	=	B5
8th fret	=	C5
9th fret	=	D♭5 (C♯5)
10th fret	=	D5
11th fret	=	E♭5 (D♯5)
12th fret	=	E5

Moveable 5th Chord
(With the Root on the 5th String)

Based on the Open A5 Chord

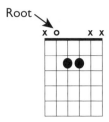

Moveable Form

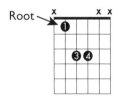

With Root At:		
1st fret	=	B♭5 (A♯5)
2nd fret	=	B5
3rd fret	=	C5
4th fret	=	D♭5 (C♯5)
5th fret	=	D5
6th fret	=	E♭5 (D♯5)
7th fret	=	E5
8th fret	=	F5
9th fret	=	F♯5 (G♭5)
10th fret	=	G5
11th fret	=	A♭5 (G♯5)
12th fret	=	A5

Moveable 6th Chord
(With the Root on the 6th String)

Based on the Open E6 Chord

Root

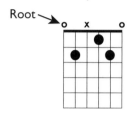

Moveable Barre Form

Root

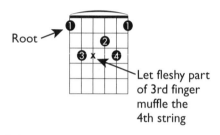

Let fleshy part
of 3rd finger
muffle the
4th string

With Root At:

1st fret	=	F6
2nd fret	=	F♯6 (G♭6)
3rd fret	=	G6
4th fret	=	A♭6 (G♯6)
5th fret	=	A6
6th fret	=	B♭6 (A♯6)
7th fret	=	B6
8th fret	=	C6
9th fret	=	D♭6 (C♯6)
10th fret	=	D6
11th fret	=	E♭6
12th fret	=	E6

Moveable 6th Chord
(With the Root on the 5th String)

Based on the Open A6 Chord

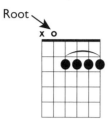

Root

x o

Moveable Barre Form

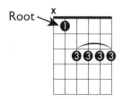

Root

x

With Root At:		
1st fret	=	B♭6
2nd fret	=	B6
3rd fret	=	C6
4th fret	=	D♭6 (C♯6)
5th fret	=	D6
6th fret	=	E♭6 (D♯6)
7th fret	=	E6
8th fret	=	F6
9th fret	=	F♯6 (G♭6)
10th fret	=	G6
11th fret	=	A♭6
12th fret	=	A6

Moveable Minor 6th Chord
(With the Root on the 6th String)

Based on the Open Fm6 Chord

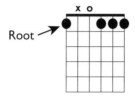

Moveable Barre Form

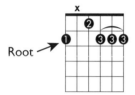

With Root At:		
2nd fret	=	F#m6 (G♭m6)
3rd fret	=	Gm6
4th fret	=	A♭m6 (G#m6)
5th fret	=	Am6
6th fret	=	B♭m6 (A#m6)
7th fret	=	Bm6
8th fret	=	Cm6
9th fret	=	D♭m6 (C#m6)
10th fret	=	Dm6
11th fret	=	E♭m6 (D#m6)
12th fret	=	Em6
13th fret	=	Fm6

Moveable Minor 6th Chord
(With the Root on the 5th String)

Based on the Open B♭m6 Chord

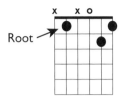

Root

Moveable Barre Form

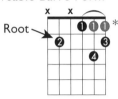

Root

Alternate Fingering
(Not Using Barre)

* ❶ = Fretted notes that do not sound

With Root At:		
2nd fret	=	Bm6
3rd fret	=	Cm6
4th fret	=	D♭m6 (C♯m6)
5th fret	=	Dm6
6th fret	=	E♭m6 (D♯m6)
7th fret	=	Em6
8th fret	=	Fm6
9th fret	=	F♯m6 (G♭m6)
10th fret	=	Gm6
11th fret	=	A♭m6 (G♯m6)
12th fret	=	Am6
13th fret	=	B♭m6 (A♯m6)

Moveable 7th Chord
(With Root on the 6th String)

Based on the Open E7 Chord

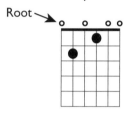

Root

Moveable Barre Form

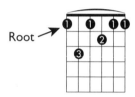

Root

With Root At:		
1st fret	=	F7
2nd fret	=	F♯7 (G♭7)
3rd fret	=	G7
4th fret	=	A♭7 (G♯7)
5th fret	=	A7
6th fret	=	B♭7 (A♯7)
7th fret	=	B7
8th fret	=	C7
9th fret	=	D♭7 (C♯7)
10th fret	=	D7
11th fret	=	E♭7 (D♯7)
12th fret	=	E7

Moveable 7th Chord
(With the Root on the 5th String)

Based on the Open A7 Chord

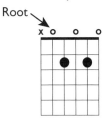

Moveable Barre Form

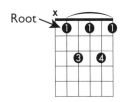

With Root At:		
1st fret	=	B♭7 (A♯7)
2nd fret	=	B7
3rd fret	=	C7
4th fret	=	D♭7 (C♯7)
5th fret	=	D7
6th fret	=	E♭7 (D♯7)
7th fret	=	E7
8th fret	=	F7
9th fret	=	F♯7 (G♭7)
10th fret	=	G7
11th fret	=	A♭7 (G♯7)
12th fret	=	A7

Moveable Major 7th Chord
(With the Root on the 5th String)

Based on Open Cmaj7 Chord

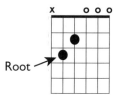

Root

Moveable Barre Form

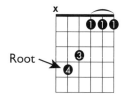

Root

With Root At:

4th fret	=	D♭maj7 (C♯maj7)
5th fret	=	Dmaj7
6th fret	=	E♭maj7 (D♯maj7)
7th fret	=	Emaj7
8th fret	=	Fmaj7
9th fret	=	F♯maj7 (G♭maj7)
10th fret	=	Gmaj7
11th fret	=	A♭maj7 (G♯maj7)
12th fret	=	Amaj7
13th fret	=	B♭maj7 (A♯maj7)
14th fret	=	Bmaj7
15th fret	=	Cmaj7

Moveable Major 7th Chord
(With the Root on the 5th String)

Based on the Open Amaj7 Chord

Root

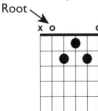

Moveable Barre Form

Root

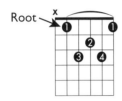

With Root At:		
1st fret	=	B♭maj7
2nd fret	=	Bmaj7
3rd fret	=	Cmaj7
4th fret	=	D♭maj7 (C♯maj7)
5th fret	=	Dmaj7
6th fret	=	E♭maj7 (D♯maj7)
7th fret	=	Emaj7
8th fret	=	Fmaj7
9th fret	=	F♯maj7 (G♭maj7)
10th fret	=	Gmaj7
11th fret	=	A♭maj7 (G♯maj7)
12th fret	=	Amaj7

Moveable Minor 7th Chord
(With the Root on the 6th String)

Based on the Open Em7 Chord

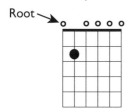

Moveable Barre Form

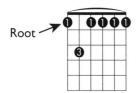

With Root At:

1st fret	=	Fm7
2nd fret	=	F#m7 (G♭m7)
3rd fret	=	Gm7
4th fret	=	A♭m7 (G#m7)
5th fret	=	Am7
6th fret	=	B♭m7 (A#m7)
7th fret	=	Bm7
8th fret	=	Cm7
9th fret	=	D♭m7 (C#m7)
10th fret	=	Dm7
11th fret	=	E♭m7 (D#m7)
12th fret	=	Em7

Moveable Minor 7th Chord
(With the Root on the 5th String)

Based on the Open Am7 Chord

Root

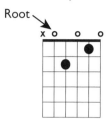

Moveable Barre Form

Root

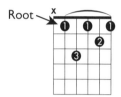

With Root At:		
1st fret	=	B♭m7 (A♯m7)
2nd fret	=	Bm7
3rd fret	=	Cm7
4th fret	=	D♭m7 (C♯m7)
5th fret	=	Dm7
6th fret	=	E♭m7 (D♯m7)
7th fret	=	Em7
8th fret	=	Fm7
9th fret	=	F♯m7 (G♭m7)
10th fret	=	Gm7
11th fret	=	A♭m7 (G♯m7)
12th fret	=	Am7

Moveable 9th Chord
(With the Root on the 6th String)

Based on the Open F9 Chord

Root

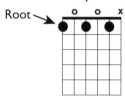

Moveable Barre Form

Root

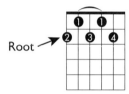

With Root At:

2nd fret	=	F#9 (G♭9)
3rd fret	=	G9
4th fret	=	A♭9 (G#9)
5th fret	=	A9
6th fret	=	B♭9 (A#9)
7th fret	=	B9
8th fret	=	C9
9th fret	=	D♭9 (C#9)
10th fret	=	D9
11th fret	=	E♭9 (D#9)
12th fret	=	E9
13th fret	=	F9

Moveable 9th Chord
(With the Root on the 5th String)

Based on the Open B♭9 Chord

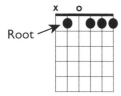

Root

Moveable Barre Form

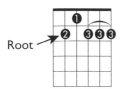

Root

With Root At:

2nd fret	=	B9
3rd fret	=	C9
4th fret	=	D♭9 (C♯9)
5th fret	=	D9
6th fret	=	E♭9 (D♯9)
7th fret	=	E9
8th fret	=	F9
9th fret	=	F♯9 (G♭9)
10th fret	=	G9
11th fret	=	A♭9 (G♯9)
12th fret	=	A9
13th fret	=	B♭9

Guitar Fingerboard Chart
Frets 1–12

STRINGS

6th 5th 4th 3rd 2nd 1st
E A D G B E

FRETS

STRINGS

Fret	6th	5th	4th	3rd	2nd	1st
← Open	E	A	D	G	B	E
← 1st Fret	F	A♯/B♭	D♯/E♭	G♯/A♭	C	F
← 2nd Fret	F♯/G♭	B	E	A	C♯/D♭	F♯/G♭
← 3rd Fret	G	C	F	A♯/B♭	D	G
← 4th Fret	G♯/A♭	C♯/D♭	F♯/G♭	B	D♯/E♭	G♯/A♭
← 5th Fret	A	D	G	C	E	A
← 6th Fret	A♯/B♭	D♯/E♭	G♯/A♭	C♯/D♭	F	A♯/B♭
← 7th Fret	B	E	A	D	F♯/G♭	B
← 8th Fret	C	F	A♯/B♭	D♯/E♭	G	C
← 9th Fret	C♯/D♭	F♯/G♭	B	E	G♯/A♭	C♯/D♭
←10th Fret	D	G	C	F	A	D
←11th Fret	D♯/E♭	G♯/A♭	C♯/D♭	F♯/G♭	A♯/B♭	D♯/E♭
←12th Fret	E	A	D	G	B	E

Fingerboard (6th 5th 4th 3rd 2nd 1st strings):

- Open: E A D G B E
- 1st Fret: F / B♭(A♯) E♭(D♯) A♭(G♯) C F
- 2nd Fret: F♯/G♭ B E A D♭(C♯) G♭(F♯)
- 3rd Fret: G C F B♭(A♯) D G
- 4th Fret: G♯/A♭ C♯/D♭ F♯/G♭ B D♯/E♭ G♯/A♭
- 5th Fret: A D G C E A
- 6th Fret: A♯/B♭ D♯/E♭ G♯/A♭ C♯/D♭ F A♯/B♭
- 7th Fret: B E A D G♭(F♯) B
- 8th Fret: C F B♭(A♯) E♭(D♯) G C
- 9th Fret: C♯/D♭ F♯/G♭ B E A♭(G♯) C♯/D♭
- 10th Fret: D G C F A D
- 11th Fret: D♯/E♭ G♯/A♭ C♯/D♭ F♯/G♭ A♯/B♭ D♯/E♭
- 12th Fret: E A D G B E